ACCOUNTING
RESEARCH METHODS
DO THE FACTS SPEAK
FOR THEMSELVES?

Wanda A. Wallace
The Deborah D. Shelton Systems Professor of Accounting
Texas A & M University

IRWIN

Homewood, IL 60430
Boston, MA 02116

©RICHARD D. IRWIN, INC., 1991

Senior sponsoring editor: *Ron Regis*
Project editor: *Karen Nelson*
Production manager: *Diane Palmer*
Cover designer: *Laurie Entringer*
Artist: Publication Services
Compositor: Precision Typographers
Typeface: *10/12 Times Roman*
Printer: *R. R. Donnelley & Sons Company*

Library of Congress Cataloging-in-Publication Data

Wallace, Wanda A.
    Accounting research methods : do the facts speak for themselves? /
Wanda A. Wallace.
        p.   cm.
    Includes index.
    ISBN 0-256-10047-0
    1. Accounting—Research—Methodology.   I. Title.
HF5630.W17 1991
657'.072—dc20   90–21373

Printed in the United States of America
1 2 3 4 5 6 7 8 9 0 DOC 8 7 6 5 4 3 2 1

To those professors, colleagues, practitioners, and students who have been particularly inspiring, with special thanks to Geraldine F. Dominiak, Thomas V. Hedges, Charles Becker, Russell M. Barefield, E. Daniel Smith, Moshe Ben-Horim, and Gary L. Holstrum

ABOUT THE AUTHOR

Wanda A. Wallace, Ph.D., CPA, CMA, CIA is the Deborah D. Shelton Systems Professor of Accounting at Texas A&M University. Dr. Wallace received the 1981 Wildman Gold Medal awarded to the most significant literary contribution to the advancement of public accounting over a three-year period by the American Accounting Association (AAA) and Deloitte Haskins & Sells. She is a coauthor of a chapter of the winner of the 1990 Wildman Gold Medal. In addition, she has two AWSCPA Literary Awards to her credit. Dr. Wallace has authored more than 10 books and monographs and over 85 articles in such journals as the *Accounting Review, Journal of Accounting Research, Auditing: A Journal of Practice & Theory, CPA Journal, Financial Executive, Harvard Business Review,* and *The Wall Street Journal.* She was awarded a Certificate of Distinguished Performance on the Certified Management Accounting Examination and the Highest Achievement Award (gold medal) on the international Certified Internal Auditor Examination.

Dr. Wallace is active in the Auditing Section of the American Accounting Association (AAA), currently serving as Editor of *The Auditor's Report.* She has recently served on a joint task force of the AICPA and Canadian Institute of Chartered Accountants, which has drafted practical guidance on applying *SAS No. 9.* Dr. Wallace chaired an Auditing Standards Advisory Council (1988–1989) to the General Accounting Office, formed by the Comptroller General of the United States. Currently, Dr. Wallace consults with national and international firms. For the past decade, she has served as Regression Consultant to the national office (and now World Firm) of Price Waterhouse, ensuring up-to-date appreciation of current practice problems. She has worked intermittently on various research projects and strategy groups with most of the other international public accounting firms. Her recent books include one directed to the professional community entitled *Handbook of Internal Accounting Controls,* published by Prentice Hall, and textbooks on *Auditing* published by Macmillan and forthcoming from PWS-Kent, as well as *Internal Auditing: Principles & Techniques* (coauthored), published by The Institute of Internal Auditors. Her *Financial Accounting* text was recently published by South-Western Publishers.

She is extremely active in the academic profession, having screened applicants for Fulbright Scholar awards from 1985 to 1988 and currently serving on the editorial board for seven national journals. She was elected in 1989 as the AAA Vice President. She has served on the resident faculty of the AAA Doctoral Consortium on two occasions, has received competitive manuscript awards from the public sector section of the AAA and the Southwest Regional Meeting of the AAA, and recently served on the program committee for the 1989 Annual Meeting of the AAA. Dr. Wallace was on the faculty of the AAA New Faculty Consortium in 1990. Professor Wallace served on the 1982–84 board of regents of the Institute of Internal Auditors and was chair of the Government and Nonprofit Section of the AAA from 1987 to 1988. Her research in auditing has been supported by four separate grants under the Peat, Marwick, Mitchell & Co.'s Research Opportunities in Auditing Program (now KPMG Peat, Marwick), by the Touche Ross Aid to Education Foundation, by a grant from the Institute of Internal Auditors Research Foundation, by a grant from the Prochnow Foundation of the Banking School of the University of Wisconsin (coauthored), and by a subcontract grant of the National Science Foundation. Her research on stock options is currently being supported by the Canadian General Accountants' Research Foundation (coauthored). Dr. Wallace has been a visiting scholar at The University of Manchester in England and the Norwegian School of Economic and Business Administration in Bergen, Norway.

PREFACE

Having developed and instructed Research Methodology I and II at the doctoral education level for the past 5 years, in tandem with an active research, teaching, and professional career of well over 15 years, I am struck by the efforts that must be expended to gain a basic understanding of research design, concepts that underlie diverse fields of inquiry, and means of sorting fact from fiction. In our information age, we must learn to be critical consumers of an ever growing product—that of facts and figures and diverse claims.

Business is increasingly dependent on research in order to remain competitive in the marketplace. Yet, unlike the sciences in which research is an integral part of most instruction, the social science nature of business and its applications orientation have too often set aside research considerations. As a result, many who are involved in critical economic and political decisions have difficulty understanding and evaluating various forms of evidence with which they are presented. If you have a curious mind, want to become a more knowledgeable consumer of information, and have aspirations of adding to our understanding through your own research, then this book is tailored to your needs.

The approach is to take a central research question and to pursue its dimensions throughout a number of chapters that describe the importance of the sort of question posed, the research design dimensions of evaluating that question, threats to the credibility of potential inferences drawn, and challenges in communication and interpretation. How various types of research could be applied to lend insights concerning the question of interest is described. Issues tied to sample selection and the role of assumptions receive special attention. A humorous account of a "fishing hole" serves as a sort of parable referent against which various representations can be evaluated. An accounting sampler of types of research performed in business characterizes both research to date and potential directions for future inquiry. The intent is to whet your appetite to pursue other sources of information on those areas of special interest.

Desired attributes of a researcher are recounted to increase understanding of what researchers do and what makes them tick, as well as to attract you to join the ranks of those curious about our world and interested in adding to our knowledge base. Implications of our information age, including a real need to fight the pollution that can prevail in such an age, are discussed in the closing chapter. The appendix and key-word index are organized with your continuing reference needs in mind.

Wanda A. Wallace

ACKNOWLEDGMENTS

As with any project of this type, a number of individuals deserve thanks. The colleagues with whom I studied at various universities, the professors who continually challenged me to think, the fellow researchers who are ever increasing the pool of knowledge from which we can draw, the practitioners who continually pose new questions that demand answers, and the students who have convinced me that this type of book would be a worthwhile investment are all to be credited.

James J. Wallace, my husband, has served as a sounding board as this project has developed. His helpful and insightful comments in keeping me on track to ensure against excessive complexity in accomplishing the goals of this project have been invaluable.

Sindy L. Rabold is my "right arm" and has seen this project through its various stages of development. Her assistance, as usual, has been indispensable.

My associates at Richard D. Irwin, particularly Lew Gossage and Ron Regis, have been supportive in making this project a reality.

To all of these individuals I extend my thanks!

W.A.W.

CONTENTS

FIGURES

CHAPTER 1

FIGHTING THE "POLLUTION" OF OUR INFORMATION AGE

October is one of the peculiarly dangerous months to speculate in stocks. The others are July, January, September, April, November, May, March, June, December, August, and February.

—*Mark Twain*[1]

The value of such investment advice from Mark Twain is questionable, though humorous. It bears out the notion that not all ideas presented constitute information.

INTRODUCTION

In this information age, we are constantly bombarded by facts and figures. One party represents that the facts clearly support his position, while another has no doubt that she can prove exactly the opposite. How is one to discern whose "facts" are to be believed? Are there not some objective criteria that can be applied to sort out fact from fiction? Moreover, if a number of facts are indeed at odds with one another, how can the relative merits of certain claims be evaluated? Can such claims be organized into a framework that can concurrently consider a number of facts and figures of differential weight?

The objective of this book is to equip you to be a more effective consumer of information. Specifically, we will revisit a framework with which you are already familiar: the scientific method. We will then discuss how research can be designed to enhance our understanding of a diverse set of questions. The relative strengths and weaknesses of such design choices will be explained. A first step in consuming information is to understand the inherent advantages and disadvantages in the design by which that information was produced.

As with most processes, the plan or design's execution is a critical facet of research. Often, when one tries to execute the best plans, unforeseen occurrences throw a wrench into the entire project and/or force an alteration to the research approach. Common problems in execution will be discussed as a means of sensitizing you, as an information consumer, to what can go wrong with the implementation of various research designs.

When research has been performed, the data obtained are analyzed and communicated with the intention of adding to our information base. This analysis, as well as the manner in which results are communicated, can be an enhancement to the overall research endeavor or actually thwart the entire process. For example, partial analyses and disclosures can be useless and often misleading. Assumptions that underlie the approaches taken to the analysis need to be carefully delineated. In addition, the extent to which these assumptions are not borne out by the data needs to be disclosed. Often, the clue in reconciling conflicting research results lies in the different assumptions that are held by each of the researchers.

Thorough communication entails a discussion of caveats and limitations and a call for future research. Such discussion is particularly useful in judging to what extent you should believe the findings. The caveats may be so pervasive that the value added by the research findings is nominal at best. However, the real challenge is to be able to generate one's own caveats, list of problems, and set of unanswered questions when these important details are omitted by the researchers, or are evaluated to be inadequate.

As we progress in becoming better consumers of information, we will concentrate on business examples. This is intentional, as economics touches all our lives and is at the core of many debates in which we have an interest and that we want resolved. As civil litigation has increased, all of us have become increasingly involved in sorting out contractual disputes and similar controversy that quickly become a pile of facts and information that we are asked to digest; jurors and litigants must understand research.

Although peculiarities exist in every specialty field, a generally accepted approach to research design, execution, analysis, and communication does exist, and it should be respected regardless of the context in which the research is being conducted. This generally accepted approach is the focal point of this book, because each of us needs to be able to filter information and determine how much credence we should attach to various facts and figures with which we are bombarded on a daily basis.

If we learn to ask the right questions, react to critical omissions and distortions, and evaluate the quality of information, then we can expect the overall quality of the facts and figures, pervasive in our daily life, to improve. As has been observed in the courtroom: "Too many use statistics as a drunk man uses a lamp-post—for support, and not for illumination."[2] Too often it appears that the saying "you get what you ask for" is descriptive of reported research results. In the absence of discriminating consumers, the popular book *How to Lie with Statistics can become a self-fulfilling prophecy, rather than an effective warning as to how statistics can be distorted.*[3] Just as disclosures have improved on packaging, through consumers' demands, disclosure of information necessary to evaluate the quality of the research that generates disparate facts and figures can and will improve through our self-education efforts. We can help fight the "pollution" of our information age by becoming better consumers.

THE SCIENTIFIC METHOD: A REMINDER

Just as numerous biology and science classes instruct throughout public education, a scientific method exists which can lead to new knowledge when properly applied. The approach is extremely intuitive and can be used in approaching virtually any problem.

'Just the Facts, Ma'm'

The first step is to understand the nature of the problem. This involves gathering facts, learning the context or frame of reference for the question at hand, and clearly delineating the scope of the intended problem-solving or research effort.

As an example, assume that you have just read an article that asserts that companies that go bankrupt typically change their financial statements' accounting methods prior to such bankruptcy. You want to evaluate the basis for such an assertion. If we place ourselves in the shoes of the researcher, we can replicate this first step of the scientific method. The researcher should become knowledgeable of basic relevant facts:

- How many companies go bankrupt?
- How much discretion do companies have in choosing among and changing their accounting methods?
- How commonplace are accounting changes?
- Are all accounting changes voluntary, or are some mandatory?
- Who would likely be affected by an accounting change, if it occurred?
- Why does someone care about an answer to this question?

The fact-finding stage can at times make the intended research a moot point. For example, if bankruptcy is too rare an event, then the likelihood of a systematic pattern emerging is greatly diminished. If accounting methods are mandated and offer few choices, then any investigation of choice becomes less interesting and potentially unworthy of study. If choice is not in the hands of the company, but is monitored by some third party, such as an auditor or board of directors, then the scope of the question enlarges. If accounting changes influence financial statements in a substantial way, then those affected would be virtually any party involved in economic transactions with that entity. This would include employees, customers, creditors, owners, regulators, prospective investors, and other interested parties whose livelihood is somewhat influenced by that entity's operations (such as bond raters, those insuring investments, and competitors).

Why someone cares is often tied to the consequences of the problem being posed. In this setting, all who have a financial interest in the disclosing company would presumably want to be able to detect any forewarning available as to the later bankruptcy of a particular entity.

Too often, research that failed to first get the facts is conducted or presented. Nonsensical results can accrue in such a setting. For example, a researcher studying municipal bond ratings did not know that municipal bond issuers can purchase insurance to guarantee payments for their bondholders and that such insurance automatically results in a top grade rating by Moody's and Standard & Poor's—two major rating agencies. The researcher found that higher-risk financial statements of municipalities, defined by performing ratio analysis, were not observed to have lower bond ratings and then questioned the effectiveness of the bond-rating process. The facts themselves could explain such a finding, since the researcher omitted consideration of a key aspect of the research context: the existence or nonexistence of bond insurance.

What Do We Already Know (or Think We Know)?

The facts, context of the problem, and scope of research provide a basis for exploring existing knowledge. What have other researchers found? Is the verdict still out, or is the evidence at hand already conclusive? If results differ from one another, is there some aspect of the conflicting information that indicates the direction for research design in future inquiry?

The idea is not to reinvent the wheel. Whether there is sufficient uncertainty to merit the expenditure of both effort and other resources to pursue further study is the question that needs to be addressed. Moreover, the research already available may suggest critical considerations in research design and execution.

Theory Development and Hypothesis Formation

Identifying the nature of the problem and the scope of inquiry, in tandem with consideration of what we already know, facilitates the formulation of a theoretical framework from which hypotheses can be formed. In the words of William Wordsworth, "Thought and theory must precede all salutary action. . . ."[4] In some cases, the theory is already developed and the research question is largely an extension of existing theoretical questions. In other cases, a theory has to be created from bits and pieces of information (inductively) or purely through conceptualization and logic (deductively), perhaps with analytics.

The development of theory will commonly require that some assumptions be invoked. When this is the case, the reasonableness of those assumptions from both a commonsense and an available-evidence perspective should be critically profiled. Although many debate how important assumptions are to a theory and whether their reasonableness is a desired or necessary attribute of the theory,[5] there seems to be consensus that model testing and enhancement often arise by relaxing assumptions and bringing assumptions more in line with reality. For example, many economic theories assume homogeneous beliefs, as though individuals agree on the direction interest rates will move or even the logical relationship of short-term and long-term interest rates. A Will Rogers' quote comes to mind: "An economist is a man that can tell you . . . what can happen under any given condition, and his guess is liable to be as good as anybody else's too."[6] While this may imply indifference among forecasts, it also suggests likely differences among such projections. By permitting nonhomogeneous expectations or beliefs, modeling has been more descriptive of segmental markets and the possibility of clientele effects on investment strategies. Such evolution is a key dimension of progress.[7]

Despite disagreement as to the relative importance of the reasonableness of assumptions in theory development and modeling versus the performance of the theory in generating useful predictions, most researchers would agree that there is a need for delineation of all key assumptions. That permits the consumers of a theory or model to evaluate for themselves whether the assumptions are acceptable.

Formulating the Research Question

In light of a particular factual setting, past research, basic common sense, and a theoretical framework, a formal research question, often referred to as a hypothesis, is formulated. A number of desirable attributes of hypotheses are described below and depicted in Figure 1.

If . . . Then

If a question is so vague as to preclude delineation of alternative findings, then the subsequent research is far less likely to produce tractable or interpretable results. One test of clarity is whether the research question can be phrased in an "if/then" form. For example, reconsider the bankrupt companies that purportedly changed accounting treatments earlier. The phrasing of the hypothesis could be:

> If a company changes its accounting methods, then bankruptcy is more likely to occur.

This phrasing is consistent with the motivation suggested earlier: the potential usefulness of observed accounting changes as signals of future financial difficulties.

The hypothesis could similarly be phrased as follows:

> If bankruptcy occurs, then the likelihood of an accounting change having been made in the recent past is more likely.

While tractable, it is far less apparent from this structure that the researcher intends to use the accounting change as a sort of predictor of bankruptcy.

By reviewing the manner in which research questions have been posed, the perspective of the researcher can be better understood, as can the likely nature of the research design and nature of findings. In the example just described, the latter phrasing would look merely at incidences of accounting changes for bankrupt companies. In contrast, the earlier phrasing would focus on companies making accounting changes and predict the relative likelihood of subsequent financial difficulties. Given the apparent signalling focus, the timing of the subsequent bankruptcy relative to the accounting change would be tracked. The nature of both the research design and the types of inferences drawn would differ substantially. The researcher has either sought to discover the quality of information on future financial difficulty that is provided by the event of an accounting change, or the researcher has focused on

FIGURE 1
Desirable Attributes of Hypotheses

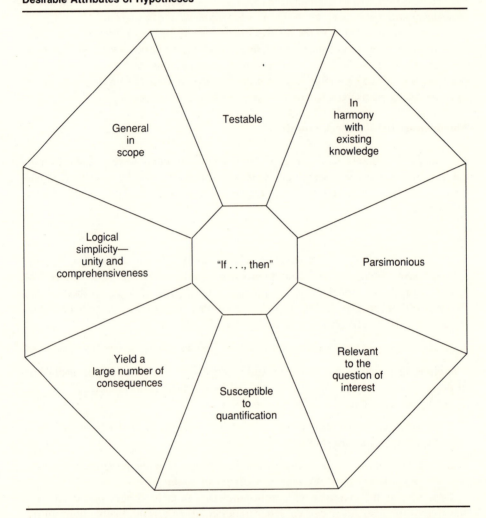

Adapted from F. J. McGuigan, *Experimental Psychology: Methods of Research*, 4th ed. (Englewood Cliffs, N.J.: Prentice Hall, 1983).

companies already bankrupt and asked what proportion of those entities previously experienced an accounting change. The problem with the latter approach from a signalling perspective is that no basis exists for determining how many "false signals" might arise—in cases where an accounting change occurs but no subsequent financial difficulties are observed.

Testable

Beyond the important directional phrasing of the "If . . . , then" wording of the hypothesis, the other attributes in Figure 1 are desirable from the point of view of enhancing the likely quality of the overall research effort. Clearly, an untestable hypothesis has no chance of being either corroborated or disputed. The sole justification for such a research question is that you believe the premise will some day be testable. Such theoretical developments lay the groundwork for future empirical inquiry, but will not increase our information base in the near future. Hence, there is a preference for testable research questions, that is, ones for which a means exists for testing their consistency with reality.

In Harmony with Existing Knowledge

The request that a hypothesis be consistent with existing knowledge merely points out that if the proposal is at odds with what is already known, in a sense, that hypothesis is already disputed. Of course, the danger exists that we do not really know some fact that is widely believed. Consider the prevailing belief that the earth was flat prior to the formation of theories and collection of evidence that the earth indeed was a sphere. Researchers must carefully define the state of "existing knowledge."

Parsimony

A desire for parsimonious hypotheses acknowledges the elegance of simplicity. The laws of supply and demand, while complex in all their nuances, are generally reduced to a set of hypotheses concerning the typical responses of consumers and suppliers to increased prices. The simpler the wording of hypotheses, the more widely understood their implications and, often, the more general their application.

Relevant to the Question of Interest

The relevancy of the hypothesis to the research question is critical and has already been addressed in our consideration of how to word the "If . . . , then" form of the research question. The evidence gathered will differ depending on the researcher's approach, and care must be taken to anticipate whether the "product" of the research is expected to be relevant to the precise research questions posed.

Susceptible to Quantification

Not only must hypotheses be testable, the matter being tested will need to be measured and quantified in some manner. While *ratio or metric scales* of measurement are superior (i.e., those that are capable of addition, multiplication, division, and proportional combinations and analyses), ordinal quantification can be evaluated. *Ordinal* refers to rankings, such as an expert's evaluation of the extensiveness of accounting change. Such a quantification may be important beyond the dollar effect of change in a single year, since accounting changes tend to have longer-term implications for measuring financial performance. Hence, an expert may well be able to compare accounting changes in terms of extensiveness of effect over a given time period, although that same expert may have difficulty quantifying that effect in dollar terms.

Some research questions result in nominal or classification results that do not rank or count. For example, the incidence of bankruptcy is a yes-or-no metric. Similarly, the incidence with which public as opposed to private companies go bankrupt is a yes-or-no result. Research tools are available for data that cannot be quantified in other than a frequency of yes/no responses. Hence, Figure 1 is not at odds with such analyses. The point of the discussion of desirable attributes is to bear out the improved power (strength) of the research design and analysis that is facilitated by use of quantifiable variables.

Yield a Large Number of Consequences

A large number of consequences are desirable because far more avenues can be investigated to test the overall model and hypotheses. Too often, several theories have similar, overlapping implications. In such cases, it is difficult to determine whether results actually support one theory or another.

Assume, for example, that a greater incidence of accounting changes is observed for bankrupt companies than for nonbankrupt companies. Also assume that when the natures of such changes are sorted in accordance with whether they are voluntary or mandatory accounting changes, the number of voluntary changes are comparable among bankrupt and nonbankrupt companies. In such a setting, it would appear that, for some reason, standard setters had been giving increased attention to accounting transactions that involved firms that eventually went bankrupt. This leads to a competing explanation for accounting changes, which is tied to standard-setting and regulatory behavior as opposed to choice by management. The implications of the two explanations are quite different, yet the consequences in terms of number of accounting changes observed among bankrupt companies are the same. In order to make inferences as to the reason that accounting changes are observed, the hypotheses related to signalling possibilities through management choice versus through standard-setting activities need to have other testable consequences. If such consequences exist, continued inquiry can begin to explain the role that accounting change plays in the eventual road to bankruptcy.

Logical Simplicity—Unity and Comprehensiveness

The logical-simplicity attribute is similar to the parsimonious attribute—both represent a desire for succinct representation of ideas. However, in the former there is a focus on the unity and comprehensiveness of the representation from a logic perspective. To be succinct at the cost of insufficient scope of analysis would be a poor trade-off. In the bankruptcy example, the scope of analysis needs to include both companies that have gone bankrupt and those that have not; otherwise, the incidence of false signals cannot be evaluated and the signalling purpose of the research inquiry cannot be addressed.

General in Scope

The more general in scope the hypothesis, the more likely it is to be applicable to a number of domains. The result is a more powerful theory and greater information value of the results. For example, the elegant theories of demand and supply in economics tend to apply to most market settings. While monopolies and predatory-pricing capabilities exist (i.e., where prices can be raised without necessarily affecting demand and where very low prices might be supported by large producers to drive out competing suppliers, despite the existence of demand at higher prices), generally speaking, one can expect demand to be dampened by higher prices and increased numbers of suppliers to enter markets where demand has increased.

Creativity

The more general implication of Figure 1 is that researchers must be creative in drafting their hypotheses. Often the process entails abstracting similarities among events observed, such as the hypothesis that bankrupt companies tend to be similar in their propensity to undergo an accounting change. Another useful tool in developing hypotheses is to form analogies. Since evidence exists that managers maneuver to buy time as they try to address problems when financial difficulties increase, an accounting change might be one analogy to such maneuvering as selling off assets or restructuring debt.

Another common approach to formulating hypotheses is to extrapolate from previous research. Often, a researcher performing a case study will describe various attributes of a company that suggest further research. For example, in analyzing a bankrupt company, details may be provided concerning how that company changed accounting practices. This observation may lead to subsequent research that considers the propensity for companies undergoing accounting changes to later have financial difficulties.

Research Design

Once the research questions have been formulated, the next step is to determine the research design. In developing such a design, a key consideration is the source of data relevant to the research question. A number of alternative sources of data are available.

Experimental Design

An experiment in the social sciences typically involves people and requires direct access by the researcher to the "*subjects.*" The means by which the researcher collects evidence might be to draft cases involving an actual judgment by the subjects as to whether a company is likely to go bankrupt. By including in the case the company attribute of having had a change in accounting, the research would provide evidence on the degree to which the "*treatment*" of an accounting change influences the variable of primary interest, the likelihood of bankruptcy. This research approach is typically referred to as a *laboratory study*.

If the researcher has access to subjects but does not plan on manipulating a treatment to infer its effect, the approach taken is referred to as a *field study*. This means that attributes are interpreted in their natural context and associations are inferred. If the experimental design is not carefully planned, the field study will become a *case study*, in which the purpose is primarily descriptive, as a basis for generating hypotheses rather than providing evidence regarding a particular research question.

Opinion Research

If the researcher is interested primarily in perceptions, as opposed to whether decisions or other actions are affected by a particular treatment, the research approach is referred to as *opinion research*. This can be performed via personal interviews, surveys, or iterative group assessments through focus groups or techniques such as the Delphi method. The *Delphi method* involves asking a group of individuals for their opinions, then sharing with the group information on the individuals' opinions, and then proceeding to ask the individuals to again form an opinion. This iterative process is repeated until reasonable consensus is reached among group members.

Archival Research

An alternative research approach is to gather data for analysis of the hypothesis. The data can be physical evidence in some lines of inquiry, or documentary evidence, such as information obtained from public filings of companies that would be expected to disclose their financial position as well as changes in accounting. The term often applied to the study of historical information is *archival research*.

Analytical Research

A major stream of inquiry not involving people or archival data is *analytical research*, which applies mathematics and logic to build models that hypothesize and proceed to prove certain types of interrelationships. Game theory can be used to model the expected behavior of managers facing financial difficulties under alternative assumptions. Such research can demonstrate the importance of monitoring practices, such as the role of an auditor, and penalty functions, such as punitive actions by regulatory bodies for fraudulent financial reporting.

An interesting and well-known illustration of game theory is known as the "prisoner's dilemma." This analytical result explains the common notion of "no honor among thieves." In the absence of collusion with full assurance of no cheating, prisoners will tend to behave in other than their joint best interests. When two prisoners are incarcerated and are presented with various cooperative arrangements, should they confess due, in large part, to suspicions about their partners, deals are often struck. The dilemma can be summarized as follows:

	The Other Prisoner Does Not Confess	The Other Prisoner Does Confess
You Do Not Confess	Both serve 1 year	You serve 10 years
You Do Confess	You serve no jail time	Both serve 9 years

This is the set of choices available to both prisoners, and each has the sole concern of minimizing the time in jail for him alone; each prisoner is aware of this dilemma facing the other (i.e., it is fully mutual).[8] The paradox is that each unilaterally, if rational, would confess and the result will be the unattractive nine years in jail. Note that the concept of what is rational choice confronts numerous decision settings, including such economic questions as when to declare bankruptcy. Game theory can help us to understand the perspective of the various thinking opponents (e.g., creditors and borrowers).

Multimethods

Each of these approaches to research can be combined with others to form *multimethod approaches*. A common example of a multimethod approach is the application of *simulation analysis*. This type of analysis uses mathematics to simulate what would happen under various conditions, but is intended to be representative of actual relationships observable in archival data. Hence, an individual building a simulation model will often first conduct archival data collection and analysis as underpinnings for the design of the model.

The idea of looking at the same research question from different perspectives by using varying research approaches is referred to as *triangulation*. Much like viewing an elephant from various directions would be expected to generate differing descriptions, varied research tools influence the picture that might result from the research approach. Hence, the application of more than one method is considered to be advantageous since it will add insights regarding the research question.

The relative strengths and weaknesses of these approaches will be the subject matter of a later chapter. At this juncture, our focus is on the evolution of the scientific method in pursuing our research question.

Method of Analysis

The research design does not only include attention to the means of collecting data or pursuing the line of inquiry analytically, but also entails a plan for analysis. The manner in which a researcher intends to analyze the data typically influences how data are collected. By the same token, constraints on the nature of available data will frequently influence the mode of analysis of such data. For example, ordinal data cannot be analyzed with the same tools as those applied to ratio data; the collection of information on the perceived extent of an accounting change along a seven-point scale will result in an analysis quite distinct from an analysis of the dollar effect of an accounting change.

If the method of analysis fails to take into account underlying assumptions and the nature of the data set or research approach, the inferences drawn will be tenuous, misleading, or erroneous. The severity of the effect of such failure, in part, will depend on the extent of departure from the assumptions or the peculiarity of the data set or approach that is not controlled.

Execution of the Research

The research is intended to be executed in a manner that is consistent with the design, but frequently problems arise that are not anticipated by the researcher. It is important that any situations not anticipated are evaluated in light of the hypothesis, assumptions, theory, and research design to ensure that some subsequent decision does not endanger the ability to produce meaningful research. As decisions are made, they need to be catalogued to ensure both a clear statement of the research approach and consistency in future decisions that arise during the research process.

The researcher should strive for damage control, whereby unforeseen problems are contained in a manner that minimizes their adverse effect on the data collection and analysis phase of the study. During the analysis phase, attention should be given to trying to quantify the likely effect of such events.

An experienced researcher will strive to anticipate the types of problems common in executing research and will plan aspects of the design to be responsive to such problems. This plan should include clear responsibility for exceptions that undoubtedly will arise regardless of how well planned the research endeavor may be.

An example of a problem that could arise in the archival research of whether companies that change accounting practices are more likely later to have financial difficulty is that certain entities may go private, precluding access to information on whether they have changed accounting practices. Such a problem will require a research design that has an adequate number of sample companies for analysis in order that the loss of some companies' data will not damage the statistical validity of inferences drawn. Moreover, the planned scope of inquiry and inference will likely be restricted to public companies for which the necessary information is available.

This and a number of other likely execution problems that interact with the various strengths and weaknesses of alternative research approaches are the subject matter of a later chapter.

Interpretation of the Findings

Once the research is executed and analyses are performed, the results are interpreted as to their implications for the research question. Specifically, is the hypothesis supported? If not supported, have possible competing hypotheses come to light through the research process? Are the findings reasonable in light of past work, expectations, common sense, and the research design's comparative strengths and weaknesses? Can inferences be drawn, and if so, is their scope constrained further than initially expected in the research design? For example, no industry bias may have been expected initially, yet, following data collection, it may be evident that the bankrupt companies are clustered in time by industry. In such a setting, the findings are far more likely to be dependent on both the time and industry under study than was anticipated in the original design.

In considering competing hypotheses, the researcher, while interpreting findings, may decide that it is important to collect more data, perform additional analyses, or extend analytical work to address other possible explanations for the research results. Such is the iterative approach to good research.

Communicating the Results

The more thorough the entire research process, the more simplified becomes the communication process. This is because the researcher will have already dovetailed the initial research idea with the formulation of the hypothesis, the specification of assumptions, the collection of data, the analysis phase, and the interpretation of findings. Caveats and competing hypotheses will have been unveiled and pursued. Unanswered questions will have been catalogued, as will potential threats to the research design and inferences drawn. The important facet of communication is that it clearly presents the distinction between a priori ideas and iterative processes, as well as both strengths and weaknesses of the particular research approach used. The inferences should be clear, along with the findings reported, and the caveats should be painstakingly disclosed. No individual should understand the strengths and weaknesses of his or her inquiry better than the researcher conducting the work. Unfortunately, researchers at times fail to allocate as much time and due care to the communication process as they do to earlier stages of the research process. Yet, that is the very stage of the work that may be widely disseminated and either used or abused in decision making.

OVERVIEW

The scientific method, familiar in its ideals, is a useful framework in which to view various research studies or modeling applications that purport to demonstrate some "fact."

When the theory is applied to test either research questions or formal research hypotheses, a number of implementation issues have to be addressed. Specifically, the type of methodology used to operationalize the research can vary across a rather broad spectrum. An experiment can be designed, a survey instrument can be distributed, a hypothetical model simulating a scenario of interest can be formulated analytically or with substantial computer replication power, historical data can be analyzed, or current data can be compared and contrasted among observational units. The choice of approach creates a number of related implementation issues, such as how an experiment is to be run, how many subjects are to be used, what the "treatment" will be, and whether there will be a control group separate from the treatment group, if a pilot test is necessary, and similar dimensions of research design.

The manner of translating theory to implementation is a critical determinant of the quality of the overall research effort. The strength of findings will vary along different dimensions, in part, because of the particular design selected. Indeed, the approach should be evaluated from a commonsense and theoretical perspective as to propriety and the potential power of the selected design in drawing conclusions. Quality control needs to be exercised when implementing a research project. Moreover, if problems are uncovered during the process, adaptation will be essential.

In the following chapters, we will focus on the strengths and weaknesses of the various decisions within the framework of the scientific method. The objective will be to sensitize you to the likely cost-benefit implications of researchers' decisions. In particular, how will their decisions influence the quality of information you read as their research is reported upon for public consumption?

CHAPTER 2

INTERNAL VALIDITY

Every increase in our knowledge results in a greater increase in the number of our problems.
—*Homer Dubs*[9]

Often what is first thought to be a simple relationship is found to be complex and comprised of five or six major elements when investigated. For example, the selection of accounting principles may be influenced by financial position, practices of an acquired company, industry norms, and constraints imposed by creditors. Hence, as the introductory quote suggests, problems mount as to how to best isolate the relative influence of any one of these elements.

At the core of evaluating research is the concept of *internal validity*. It asks the question of whether the researcher has successfully isolated the effect of a particular treatment. In other words, is it the treatment observed or manipulated that resulted in the difference noted in the variable of interest? In a laboratory experiment, the intent is to infer causality, that is, that the treatment actually caused a particular outcome. Returning to the bankruptcy laboratory study described earlier, the intent would be to demonstrate how the treatment of an accounting change having occurred affects the subject's judgment that bankruptcy was likely. If those subjects who were given the same case facts with the absence of an accounting change systematically assessed bankruptcy to be less likely than those subjects who were also told of the accounting change, then the expected interpretation would be one of causal linkage.

However, a number of threats to the internal validity of the laboratory study can be anticipated. These threats are diagrammed in Figure 2, and their description is the subject matter of this chapter.

INSTRUMENTATION

The first threat relates to how the experiment is actually executed in terms of *instrumentation* or measurement. For example, if subjects in a lab experiment are provided different instruments to formulate and communicate their decisions, this difference in instrumentation could become the unintended treatment, rather than the element of real interest, which is the change in accounting method. In the lab experiment, a case has been developed in which two groups of subjects were given identical information except for the change in accounting, which was omitted from the information given to one

FIGURE 2
Internal Validity Threats (Risks in assessing whether the experimental treatment makes a difference)

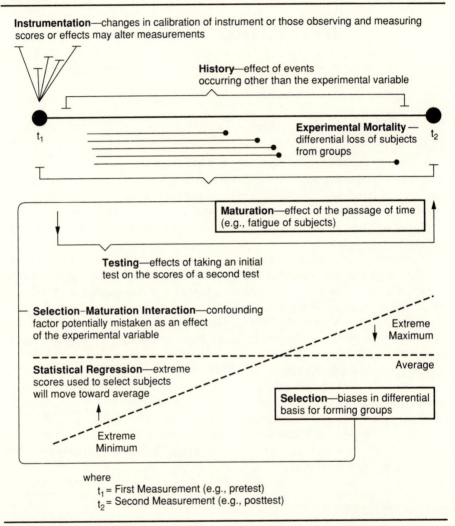

Instrumentation—changes in calibration of instrument or those observing and measuring scores or effects may alter measurements

History—effect of events occurring other than the experimental variable

t_1

Experimental Mortality—differential loss of subjects from groups

t_2

Maturation—effect of the passage of time (e.g., fatigue of subjects)

Testing—effects of taking an initial test on the scores of a second test

Selection–Maturation Interaction—confounding factor potentially mistaken as an effect of the experimental variable

Extreme Maximum

Statistical Regression—extreme scores used to select subjects will move toward average

Average

Selection—biases in differential basis for forming groups

Extreme Minimum

where
t_1 = First Measurement (e.g., pretest)
t_2 = Second Measurement (e.g., posttest)

Adapted from Donald T. Campbell and Julian C. Stanley, *Experimental and Quasi-Experimental Designs for Research* (Chicago: Rand McNally, 1963), p. 5.

group. A lot of research, however, will strive to not only make comparisons *between subjects*, but also *within subjects*. Such research would compare decisions of the same individual. In order to elicit responses to make comparisons within subjects, multiple cases would have to be developed to vary the treatment and yet not make the treatment too transparent. This may lead to the use of different companies in different industries within such cases, creating unintended effects on individuals' bankruptcy judgment, beyond the mere effect of the change in accounting.

Beyond the instrument prompting a judgment is the question of how the subject is asked to respond. Are subjects asked to answer yes or no (that is, bankruptcy is expected or not expected), or do we ask what is the probability of failure? When eliciting probability judgments, many approaches are possible, some of which can produce substantial instrumentation effects. For example, a researcher might have some instruments with a line extending from 0 percent to 100 percent and merely request the respondent to mark the probability on the line. Other instruments might require the subject to write a percentage on a blank line. Another instrument might have a 1- to 5-point scale (often referred to as a *Likert scale*) where 1 indicates no chance of bankruptcy, 3 means that the subject is uncertain, and 5 signals probable bankruptcy. For such an instrument, the meaning of the subjects' responses becomes a problem: What do people mean by "no," "remote," "possible," or "probable"?

Due to some individuals' inability to think probabilistically without some assistance, some researchers will elicit feedback in an interview situation. One popular tool is a colored wheel that uses a red background to indicate no likelihood. The researcher slowly uncovers the wheel until the subject indicates that the exposed portion of the wheel represents the likelihood envisioned by him or her for some event. While this approach uses visual aids quite effectively and has been demonstrated to be easier for people to interpret due to its "pie-slice" approach to probabilistic judgment, a number of threats to internal validity arise. For example, each interviewer may have a different style in using the visual aid, and this difference among interviews could create systematic differences in measurement that are unrelated to the particular treatment under study. The individual recording the portion of the circle indicating the likelihood of a certain event may also not be consistent when taking measurements for different subjects.

The instrumentation problem can be constrained by minimizing variations in research instruments used to gather information, using a single individual to gather the information with as precise a measurement tool as is possible, and striving to maximize the consistency of that individual by avoiding fatigue, long lapses of time between measurements, and other factors that could lead to measurement variations unintended by the researchers.

These means of constraint may themselves threaten the ability to make generalizations based on the research results. For example, the case may have involved a particular industry that in and of itself might have evoked the different reactions from subjects, meaning that this response may by no means hold for other industries. The use of a single interview fails to guard against the possibility of systematic errors in that researcher's approach; this precludes replication and makes generalizations impossible. In other words, multiple data collectors can serve as a sort of monitoring device on the data-collection process, although they may concurrently introduce errors.

The extent to which instrumentation effects influence decisions can be an explicit plank in research design. For example, multiple instrumentation could be used and then comparisons made as to the resiliency of results across such variations. By assessing the exposure to measurement or case instrument variations, greater assurance will be gained that observed effects over and above such exposure are more likely to be tied to the treatment of interest. The consistency among those collecting data and within subjects can be evaluated as well, again with the purpose of quantifying the threat posed by instrumentation.

HISTORY

The effects of events that occur other than the effect of the experimental variable are referred to as *history threats* to internal validity. Specifically, if during the execution of the research, a subject muttered "this looks bad," that utterance, rather than the intended treatment, may have elicited a response by other subjects. By the same token, if a break were permitted during the experiment and subjects spoke with one another, then such conversations may influence the result. If the research were conducted over several days and some subjects happened to watch a business news report that mentioned that bankruptcy was on the upsurge, leading to responses that are different from earlier ones, the change in responses could be wrongly attributed to the treatment in the case.

History threats can be constrained by shortening the time involved in the data collection, trying to control for outside factors (e.g., restricting influence from the media and precluding interaction among subjects), and maintaining as uncontaminated a laboratory environment as is possible. However, such constraints can introduce other threats, such as restricted scope of inquiry, subjects' fatigue, and unnatural settings for evaluation. Indeed, some may challenge whether the decision at hand would ever be made by an individual based merely on the information sources provided without other information-search activities, including conversations with knowledgeable colleagues.

EXPERIMENTAL MORTALITY

In the course of executing research, subjects may be lost for a variety of reasons, and this loss may not be proportionately distributed throughout the sample under study. For example, the subjects that drop out of the experiment could all be those subjects who were informed of a change in accounting principle, rather than half from that group and half from the other, that is, the *control group* (the group not receiving the treatment and serving as a benchmark to which comparisons will be made). Care must be taken not to attribute the change in result that is due to the change in the composition of the group to the treatment effect under study.

Experimental mortality can also be minimized by shortening the time period over which data are collected. This avoids the likelihood of illness or death causing individuals' participation in the study to end. The effects of such a problem can be further controlled by selecting more subjects than required for the study's results to be valid, as a sort of buffer zone to avoid the effect of loss of subjects. Of course, the same sorts of ill effects from controlling for history can arise from some of the steps taken to avoid experimental mortality. In addition, some experiments require that time elapses before collecting additional information. When faced with such a demand by the nature of the research question, experimental mortality can be particularly threatening since subjects may not only leave for unavoidable purposes but may also simply lose interest.

MATURATION

In an experiment that spans some length of time, *maturation* of subjects could be a threat to internal validity. This means that the effect of the passage of time is being measured instead of the effect of the intended treatment. For example, a particularly long experiment can result in subjects becoming fatigued and their judgments being influenced rather than the influence of the various treatments being measured.

Maturation problems are principally addressed by limiting the actual time taken by the experiment. As a result, the researcher may have to sacrifice certain controls, replications, tests of instrumentation, and preferable design attributes. However, maturation problems must be balanced against such benefits, or else the entire inquiry can be undermined simply because the subjects are too tired to participate fully in the experimental task.

TESTING

Researchers often use a *pretest/posttest approach* to evaluating the role of a treatment, but a risk exists that the very testing process causes differences in response, rather than the variable of interest. The question is whether the subject would have given the same response to the second test in the absence of the first test. Moreover, unintended influences of that first test could distort the findings and lead to unintended inferences.

In the bankruptcy lab experiment, the within-subject comparisons might well include a case without the change in accounting principle and the case with that principle. At times, one can document *order effects*, whereby those subjects first given the "without a change in principle" instrument actually perform differently from those who received that instrument last. This would suggest some threat to the internal validity merely due to the ordering of the initial "test."

One means of avoiding *testing effects* is to design the experiment in a manner that has groups with no pretest or within-subject comparison possibility for analysis, parallel to those with a pretest, varying the order of such tests randomly. These steps will facilitate measurement of the testing effects and/or randomize such noise to avoid systematic effects on the results obtained.

SELECTION

The *selection of subjects* can result in biases that change the results and are improperly attributed to the treatment. For example, if the selection of subjects failed to guard against previous experiences with bankruptcy and differentially sized companies, and it happened that subjects given the cases with a change in accounting principle had prior experience with bankruptcy and were mainly experienced with smaller companies, then their assessment of increased likelihoods of bankruptcy could easily be linked to their past experience rather than to the treatment effect intended.

Random selection of subjects (i.e., where every person has an equal likelihood of selection) is virtually impossible in executing research. The pool of subjects to which a researcher has access is often a function of geographical proximity, willingness to participate, student status, or some similar attribute that may well lead to systematic differences between the subjects under study and those in the general population. An important step in the research process is to collect demographic information on the subjects, believed to be potentially relevant to the research questions being examined (but not in a transparent manner), to facilitate later analysis of whether such attributes influenced the responses obtained in any systematic way.

Since random selection of subjects is commonly precluded, the next-best alternative often invoked in experimental research is *random assignment of the subjects* to the groups under study. In other words, each subject has an equal chance of being assigned to the group receiving the experimental treatment as he or she does to being assigned to the control group. Although this does begin to address the problem of selection biases within the sample, it does nothing to ensure that the sample initially selected is representative of the population for which the researcher wishes to make generalizations. This concern is the subject matter of Chapter 3.

STATISTICAL REGRESSION

If the selection of subjects is based on a criterion such as extreme scores on a test instrument, then a threat is posed to internal validity in the form of *statistical regression*. This term refers to the tendency of extreme scores to move toward the average. In other words, those receiving extreme minimum scores will tend to move upward toward the average and those receiving extreme maximum scores will likewise begin to move down toward the average. If a researcher were to select subjects based on their extreme probability assessments as to the propensity for bankruptcy, for example, too low, then one might attribute an increased probability assessment to the treatment of a reported change in accounting principle when, in fact, the increase was merely a predictable statistical regression effect.

The researcher should either avoid such extremes as the primary determinant of participation or assess via a control group what portion of the shift is attributable to this statistical regression effect.

SELECTION-MATURATION INTERACTION

Another substantial threat to internal validity stems from the possibility of an *interaction effect between selection criteria and maturation*. Specifically, the possibility exists of a confounding factor potentially being mistaken as an effect of the experimental variable. As an example, if the study of judgments on the propensity to have financial failure were conducted using a control group comprised of students of one professor and a treatment group consisting of students of another professor, and the experiment were performed in two or three stages, then the possibility exists (1) that the group taught by one professor is systematically different from the other group due to self-selection practices with respect to course enrollment and (2) that the lectures and other effects of different professors, including assignments and discussions among class members, could create some effect that is misinterpreted as a treatment effect. Randomly assigning students from the two classes to control and treatment groups would be one means of avoiding this interaction, although the ability to generalize beyond the two classes would still be an issue.

CONSIDERING INTERNAL VALIDITY THREATS IN ARCHIVAL RESEARCH

While laboratory experiments often manipulate treatments and infer causality, many archival studies search for association and systematic movement between variables of interest on which data are collected post facto. Consider the possibility that the research into the bankruptcy question proceeds as follows:

> The researcher identifies a random sample of companies and explores whether or not a change in accounting principle has been adopted by the companies in a time period spanning five years. After sorting the sample into those companies that instituted a change in accounting principle and those who did not, the researcher quantifies the incidence of bankruptcy over the following five-year time frame.

This archival approach tests whether an association exists between a change in accounting principle and the propensity for bankruptcy. Although an association, rather than a causal link, is being observed, concerns for internal validity still apply. The question merely shifts slightly to whether the association being quantified links the two events of interest, that is, the analogy to a treatment—the change in accounting principle—and the effect of interest—the propensity for later bankruptcy.

Instrumentation

Consider the sources for the various threats to internal validity and how they manifest themselves in the context of an archival research project directed at the bankruptcy question of interest. With respect to instrumentation, the question arises of what constitutes an accounting change. Are we talking only about accounting changes that are flagged with some language of inconsistency in the auditor's report? What if the financial statements have been retroactively restated due to a pooling of interests (merger) between two companies? What if, rather than a change in principle, a change is deemed to be a change in estimate and hence is handled differently from the typical accounting principle change? What if the change is not in accounting principle at all but relates to changes in estimates such as the life of assets in use? Technical details about what constitutes a change in accounting become critical in the instrumentation process. If different information sources are used or different research assistants collect the information from annual reports by the companies, measurement differences can arise that could contaminate the ability to draw inferences regarding the association of interest.

A similar problem arises in the instrumentation of bankruptcy, since a variety of definitions have been used in past research. Not only are there different types of bankruptcy, there is also the question of how a reorganization, a restructuring of debt, or a technical noncompliance with a loan covenant should be handled? What constitutes later financial difficulty to which the researcher wishes to draw an inference? Once again, if differing definitions are applied either by the data sources or by those collecting information from various sources, a threat to internal validity will arise.

History

A history effect of obvious influence would be a change in bankruptcy law or reporting and accounting practices. As mentioned earlier, mandatory changes in accounting could stem from variations in standard setting rather than individual managers' choices. A number of cyclical and seasonal effects could influence a company's operations over a five-year window beyond the influence of a change in accounting principle. How can the effects of such other historical factors be sufficiently controlled to isolate the treatment of interest?

The response of researchers is often to use a model that controls for extraneous factors or to form a matched sample that similarly tries to set aside other factors. Specifically, a model in which the incidence of bankruptcy is related to the incidence of accounting changes could also control for attributes such as the size of the company, its industry, its stock market performance, its capital structure, its ownership attributes (e.g., closely held), and its auditor. Alternatively, when selecting the sample to be analyzed, for every entity observed to have a change in accounting principle, the research could attempt to identify another company of similar size, in the same industry, and with similar capital structure to serve as a member of the control group. In such a manner, the size, industry, and capital structure effects would presumably be implicitly controlled.

A problem with the *matched-sample approach* is that the selection process precludes any assessment of the importance of size, industry, or capital structure to the question at hand. Hence, the ability to generalize findings is often damaged. Similarly, in the modeling approach, the problem persists that not every aspect of history of potential importance has been identified and controlled in the model. Further, the means of measuring the effects of interest may be faulty. For example, should size be measured as total sales dollars, total assets, or total number of employees? Perhaps some other size metric is more relevant. Since these measurement difficulties similarly apply to the matched-sample approach, the possibility exists of the measurement error mixing with the association of real interest; in other words, all of the effects of size, industry, and capital structure may not have been effectively controlled via the matching process. A very difficult task in executing a matched-sample approach is striving to be certain that the control and treatment companies are sufficiently close together on the attributes of interest. Can two companies with a gap of $5 million in sales still be regarded as properly matched? What about a gap of $100 million?

Experimental Mortality

In the study at hand, mortality of companies is part of the research question, but it is to occur in the later five-year period. What happens if the bankruptcy occurs the year after the change in accounting principle that was instituted in the fifth year of the five-year period for which information is obtained on accounting changes? What if a company shifts from public to private status, as mentioned earlier, and data on the control variables such as size and capital structure are no longer available? What if the company under study merges with another?

Much past research has been criticized for suffering from a *survivorship bias* because by definition failed companies tend to be pruned out of the analysis of companies due to unavailable information. If mergers often involve acquisition of troubled companies requiring working capital, they too seem to systematically get culled from the companies under analysis. These effects could cause the improper attribution of an effect of accounting change when none would apply if the original sample could have been kept intact. Perhaps more likely in this setting is the possibility of finding no association when one indeed existed but could not be assessed due to the factors of acquisition and premature bankruptcy from a perspective of the research design proposed.

When unable to control the effect of a threat to internal validity, the researcher will often purposefully select the sample in a manner that works against finding an association. The reason is that such a strategy prevents a third party from attributing the association to the internal validity threat. Instead, the point must be granted that the association must be even stronger than quantified, because the researcher, by design, weakened the measurement of that association.

Maturation

The passage of time can have an untold number of effects on the subject companies. For example, they may have grown, retrenched, differentially responded to a stock market crash or extreme change in interest rates, and been differentially affected by political actions influencing taxes or other regulatory factors. If it happened that financially troubled companies also had higher debt levels and faced increased interest rates, then inferences drawn about the role of changes in accounting principles may be dependent on the presence of higher borrowing rates.

Testing

In a sense, a two-stage test arises here, one stage that filters the existence of an accounting change and one stage that assesses the incidence of bankruptcy. Since two distinct periods are being defined and data demands are imposed for various control factors, the effects of the first stage on the second stage could outweigh the effects of the attribute of interest. Whenever screening is necessary or data availability constraints apply, care should be taken in drawing inferences. One interesting observation has been made in the literature that many researchers have restricted their studies to companies that have a December year-end. As a result, entire industries such as retailing are virtually precluded from analysis. Moreover, December year-end companies are larger, have lower risk, and are more likely to be regulated than are companies with a different fiscal year-end. Such findings suggest limitations to attempts to generalize studies that narrow their attention to December year-end companies.[10] This type of factor can be viewed as a pretest effect or as a selection bias effect, but whatever the classification is, the result is a threat to internal validity.

Selection

The *selection bias* merges with the testing effects in the proposed study but is clearly of a selection bias nature in phase one's restriction. Specifically, the study will be restricted to public companies that existed in the earlier five-year period. Private companies, newer industries such as computer technology and software companies, and smaller entities that are often underrepresented in various public databases will no doubt be precluded from analysis. If it happened that the basis on which phase one is executed is linked to either the incidence of bankruptcy or the frequency of accounting change, then the internal validity of the study is again threatened.

Statistical Regression

Some researchers focusing on financial difficulty will drive their sample selection process using a filter such as the *Altman Z-score*[11] or similar measure of the propensity to go bankrupt. The idea is that this filter identifies financially troubled firms that can be the focus for looking at some factor of interest, such as the incidence of accounting changes. However, the Altman Z-score will produce extremes, as does any algorithm, which over time will approach the mean. Hence, if subject companies in either the treatment or control group were selected based on their scores on a scale intended to describe propensity for bankruptcy, then a movement in the opposite direction could easily be a statistical artifact rather than a real change in probabilities tied to the intended treatment.

The advantage of *using a filter* such as a set of ratios that signify financial difficulty is that the subject companies are more relevant to the research question being posed and hence more likely to be affected. The idea is to "blow up" the effect of interest so that it can be measured and worry about competing hypotheses and the ability to generalize in future research. While such an approach can be justified at times, considerable care must be exercised in its interpretation and communication to guard against others drawing inappropriate conclusions.

Selection-Maturation Interaction

Consider the possibility that the Z-score was applied and as a result the subject companies tended to have high amounts of debt in their capital structure, and during the time frame under study, interest rates rose. In such a setting, the attribution of increased propensity for bankruptcy would likely be linked to the capital structure and borrowing rates rather than any incidence of changes in accounting practices. This is the interaction effect alluded to earlier that could make the results very time-dependent and sample-specific in nature.

THE TYPICAL TRADE-OFF

Generally, a laboratory experiment will have a greater degree of internal validity than other research approaches such as field studies or archival inquiries. This is due to the ability of a researcher to manipulate the treatment, control the other factors influencing the subject, and presumably constrain the time required for the experiment to avoid many of the threats to internal validity. As one moves away from an experimental setting, the various threats grow and one consequence is that causality cannot be tested, only association. This is due to the inability of the researcher to vary the treatment; instead, the researcher has to work with naturally occurring phenomena and structure a *quasi-experimental design* to assess patterns of interest.

CHAPTER 3

EXTERNAL VALIDITY

> [I]t is statistically true that there have been no forest fires on Manhattan Island since the
> "Smokey the Bear" advertisements have been displayed in New York subways. However,
> it is not commonly accepted that this statistic proves the value of advertising.[12]

Research is said to have *external validity* when the findings based on the sample under study can be generalized. No doubt, forest fires have persisted in the Northwest despite the advent of "Smokey the Bear" ads. In other words, the Manhattan Island observation cannot be generalized. When such is the case, external validity is lacking. Indeed, in this case, a spurious association has been inappropriately interpreted as a causal linkage. Now apply the goal of external validity to our hypothetical inquiry on bankruptcy.

The objective in the proposed research on the linkage of changes in accounting principles to the incidence of bankruptcy is to draw inferences to companies that are not included in the actual study. The intent is for the sample companies to be representative of the broader population of companies from which they are drawn. Moreover, the inferences drawn for the particular time frame defined would presumably apply to other time periods. In the case of the experimental lab approach, the manner in which the treatment is observed to have influenced subjects' decisions is expected to similarly influence other decision makers. The intent is to gain an understanding that would apply in real-life settings, not merely in the laboratory for the specific case instrument used in the experiment.

A number of threats to external validity can damage the ability to generalize based on a particular research effort. Each of these threats is depicted in Figure 3. This chapter will explain the nature of these threats and illustrate how they might be present in research related to bankruptcy projection, based on the incidence of changes in accounting principles.

SAMPLE FINDINGS

The possibility exists that research will produce sample-specific findings. This can be the result of a nonrepresentative sample selection process or the fact that the unusual combination of various internal validity problems has led to peculiar results for the

FIGURE 3
External Validity Threats

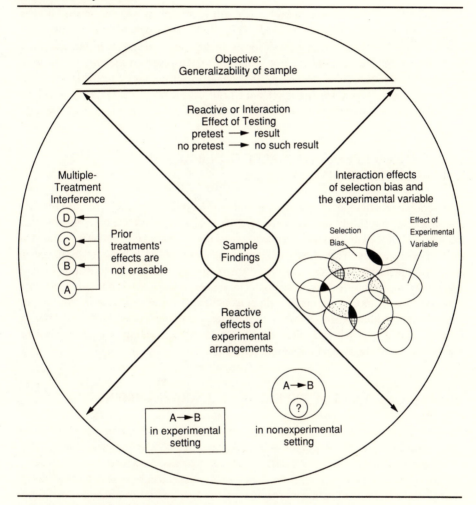

Adapted from Donald T. Campbell and Julian C. Stanley, *Experimental and Quasi-Experimental Designs for Research* (Chicago: Rand McNally, 1963), pp. 5–6.

specific research project. In the laboratory study of how a case study's treatment effect of a change in accounting principle relates to a decision regarding the propensity for bankruptcy, the subjects might all be students and lack any generalization to actual investors. Alternatively, the professor's effect on those particular students may even constrain one from generalizing to other students.

REACTIVE OR INTERACTION EFFECT OF TESTING

The possibility exists that with a pretest a result is observed, whereas in the absence of a pretest no such result is observed. This would be evidenced if a test group in which no within-subject variation was sought had different reactions to the change in accounting principle than did the test group for which *repeated measures* were used (i.e., several iterations of a case study). If a change in accounting principle is perceived as relevant only when it was missing from a prior case analysis, then this may well be an artifact of the experiment rather than a meaningful influence on decision making.

INTERACTION EFFECTS OF SELECTION BIAS AND THE EXPERIMENTAL VARIABLE

A selection bias can interact with the variables of interest to the researcher in a manner that precludes the ability to generalize to other subjects. As an example, assume that the selection of the laboratory experiment's subjects was based on volunteers interested in accounting topics. These individuals may be predisposed to react to a change in accounting principle, whereas a typical decision maker without an inclination toward accounting would not similarly react to the treatment. Comparably, if the *self-selection process* attracted more individuals with personal experiences related to bankruptcy or small business failure, their expectations with respect to the propensity for bankruptcy in the presence of disclosures that there has been an accounting change may not be representative of the typical individual's expectations.

REACTIVE EFFECTS OF EXPERIMENTAL ARRANGEMENTS

At times, the mere fact that subjects are placed in a laboratory setting creates an effect of a treatment or an outcome that would not appear in a nonexperimental setting. This can arise for a variety of reasons. First, the subjects may assume a sort of game mentality and strive to please the experimenter.[13] In a sense, the subject tries too hard to please the researcher, and the instrument may be too transparent and facilitate such artificial behavior. Second, the instrument may overstate the relative weighting of cues and misrepresent the extent to which other factors could possibly remain constant. This arises from simplifying decision settings, forcing certain attributes to remain unchanged when, in actuality, they would move with the treatment, or designing an instrument so that associations among variables are manufactured or omitted, relative to the real-world context. Any of these flaws in instrument design may result in a well-controlled experiment of virtually no relevance outside of that particular setting.

In the case at hand, subjects may figure out through multiple case studies that certain attributes are being changed while most remain the same and then try to assign some meaning to those factors that change. As a result, they may alter their projections regarding the incidence of bankruptcy when faced with a change in accounting principle, primarily to help produce an experimental result. Their intention is not to undermine the research, but rather to help produce what is viewed to be a successful experiment. Yet, ironically, the result is that the experiment is ruined from the point of view of drawing meaningful inferences to other settings and to actual decisions.

MULTIPLE-TREATMENT INTERFERENCE

In research, whatever treatments have already been manipulated cannot be erased and these prior treatments may interfere with one another. As a result, the findings may fail to generalize to settings in which the other treatments are not present or in which treatments are not ordered in a similar manner. In a within-subjects design where an individual is asked to review several scenarios and project bankruptcy, the fact that bankruptcy has already been selected as probable may reduce any possibility of later manipulations, including a change in accounting principle, having any effect. This fact illustrates how important the case study itself is as a treatment even before specific factors are manipulated. It also illustrates that in an experimental setting it is fairly easy for a task to be transparent so that a subject focuses on what has changed among cases, and, as with the reactive effect of the experimental arrangements per se, order effects arise and experimental artifacts result.

CONSIDERING EXTERNAL VALIDITY IN
ARCHIVAL RESEARCH

External validity threats apply to archival research in a similar fashion as they arise in laboratory research. Reconsider the examination of companies over a five-year time period to quantify the incidence of accounting changes and then the focus on a later five-year period to assess the incidence of bankruptcy. The question is whether the results from such a study could be generalized.

Sample Findings

As previously suggested in describing the likely selection bias of the proposed study, the possibility arises that the sample could not be generalized to the population of companies because of the virtual absence of certain segments of the market, such as newer companies, merged companies, and those companies that have gone private. However, a larger threat is presented by the idea that the selection process, particularly if a matched sampling approach were superimposed on the control and treatment groups, could produce such a peculiar sample that the observed associations were in fact peculiar to the sample at hand. This could happen if matching precluded certain industries' inclusion due to their dominance by conglomerates or their concentration serving as a barrier to matching along the size dimension.

Reactive or Interaction Effect of Testing

The presumption that the Altman Z-score or some similar filter highlights the propensity for bankruptcy creates a possibility that without such a filter the association observed in the research would not have emerged. This would suggest that the samples identified through the Z-score are not representative of the broader population of companies at large.

Interaction Effects of Selection Bias and the Experimental Variable

The possibility exists that the Z-score used for filtering creates a systematic effect of a change in accounting principle that would not be observed in the absence of the selection criterion. In such a setting, the results would not be applicable to entities that failed to register a certain Z-score. If public company status influences the propensity to go bankrupt, then a selection approach restricted to public companies may result in an association being detected between a change in accounting principle and the propensity to go bankrupt that would not be applicable to other companies.

Reactive Effects of Experimental Arrangements

The experimental setting for archival research is commonly the context of the model or matched sample. Often, tests of hypotheses are *joint tests* of the model in which the treatment is embedded and the association of such treatment with the variable of interest, in this case the propensity to go bankrupt. If the model has variables with measurement errors or omits factors that need to be controlled, then the associations estimated in the context of the model may not be observable in other contexts. Since the relevant range of a model is defined by the variable set used to estimate the relationships, the possibility exists that the relevant range estimated will not be sufficiently broad to apply to the companies to which the researcher wishes to draw generalizations.

Multiple-Treatment Interference

Just as pretests and selection bias can interact with the propensity to go bankrupt, various treatments may influence the association between bankruptcy and changes in accounting principles. In a research design that considers a window of five years, the possibility exists of prior treatments, such as a technical default on a bond covenant or a restructuring of debt, influencing the association observed between bankruptcy and the change in accounting principle. A problem in modeling that can arise is a *proxy effect*, where one variable thought to measure a certain dimension is actually proxying for some other effect. In the setting just described, if it happened that all companies with a change in accounting principle also happened to have had a technical default on bond covenants, then attributing bankruptcy to the change in accounting principle would be inappropriate. In fact, the association might well exist with the technical default, rather than the change. If the general population of companies does not similarly have the coexistence of technical defaults and changes in accounting principles, then the associations observed in the sample under study would not be observed if companies not in the sample are studied.

THE TYPICAL TRADE-OFF

Generally, an archival study will have a greater degree of external validity than other research approaches, such as a laboratory experiment, simulation, or analytical model. This is due to the use of actual empirical data on companies, rather than a facsimile of actual information, as is typical in a laboratory experiment.

One of the key factors believed to harm the external validity of research in a laboratory setting is the *motivation of subjects*. If a research project is striving to assess the influence of some factor on an assessment of the probability of bankruptcy, the challenge is to have decision makers take the experiment as seriously as they would a real-life assessment. How to motivate decisions analogous to a loan officer's actual evaluation of borrowers, when real money is involved, or to an investor's evaluation of investment alternatives, is the open question. This question concerning the subject, who is the source of data, is amusingly addressed in a commentary on pollsters' surveys:

> Public agencies are very keen on amassing statistics—they collect them, add them, raise them to the nth power, take the cube roots and prepare wonderful diagrams. But what you must never forget is that every one of those figures comes in the first instance from the village watchman, who just puts down what he damn pleases.[14]

In a simulation or mathematical model, the threat to external validity arises from the possibility that the assumptions and relationships defined in such analyses are at odds with reality. While the mathematical computations may be appropriately defined, if they are premised on faulty assumptions, then the predictability of that model becomes suspect.

CHAPTER 4

SAMPLE SELECTION

Far better an approximate answer to the right question, which is often vague, than an exact answer to the wrong question, which can always be made precise.

—John Tukey[15]

The quote above points to the importance of knowing the question of interest before selecting a sample. Without such direction, a very large sample can nonetheless generate a precise meaningless conclusion. A major source of many of the internal and external validity threats detailed in Chapters 2 and 3 relate to the manner in which the sample to be studied is selected. Often, the quality of the information obtainable from a research project is most related to the nature of the sample selected for the inquiry. A frequently used term is *random selection*. The goal of random selection is that no pattern is intended to emerge from the selection of sampling units, be they individual companies or people who serve as subjects in the investigation. However, the meaning of *random* can only be interpreted relative to the population to which it applies.

POPULATION DETERMINATION

The *population* is that set of items or individuals from which a sample is to be drawn. By definition, the sample can only be statistically inferred to be representative of that population from which it is drawn. Often, analogies are nonetheless drawn in a judgmental manner (not statistically based) on the premise that little reason exists to expect systematic differences in the population tested and other populations of interest. The populations to which consumers of research wish to draw inferences should be an important consideration in determining the population to be tested.

Common sense is the first tool to invoke in this decision process. If the research question, such as propensity to disclose changes in accounting principles, requires that information be available on accounting practices that has a reasonable level of credibility, the researcher may deem public companies that are audited as being the relevant population of interest. If the inquiry is directed to investors on a particular stock exchange, such as the New York Stock Exchange, then that population will be the relevant group from which samples will be drawn. Note, however, that the assertion that the New York Stock Exchange is representative of over-the-counter companies' practices can easily be challenged. Hence, if investors in smaller companies sought information on the bankruptcy-prediction power of changes in accounting principles, a different approach would have to be taken to defining the population.

An area of considerable controversy is whether samples drawn from the population of college students can be expected to be representative of various decision makers in the more general population or in various professions. Generally speaking, the consensus would seem to be that a mental process, presumably common to human subjects with a similar level of education, should be testable on students as representative of other groups. However, mental processes that are directed to professional expertise or are likely to be influenced by the subjects' vested interest, are probably not effectively captured by studies focusing on student subjects.

The literature is replete with examples of poor definitions of populations to be sampled. A presidential election in the United States that was misjudged in large part because only people with telephones were sampled is perhaps the most infamous example of polling that was unrepresentative.[16] When the U.S. media conduct polls in other countries that are at odds with local polls and outcomes, as has happened in both Central America and Eastern Europe, whether the willingness of individuals to be polled by American media representatives constitutes a selection bias in and of itself is a question that must be raised.

Some studies in business have been geographically focused due to the high cost of travel and comparative advantages in gaining local businesses' cooperation. Specifically, a study of lending officers in Chicago was claimed to be potentially relevant to the entire population of lending officers, since no clear reason existed to expect a systematic difference in decision making. This poses the challenge for the researcher to think through competing claims and how they might be addressed. For example, if Chicago banks are more likely to have portfolios comprised of different types of loans than other parts of the country, decisions could well be influenced differentially by this distinctive experience. In particular, Southwest banks may have oil-related investments as a substantial part of their portfolios, leading to different approaches in evaluating risk and deciding portfolio composition.

Consider how your reaction would be altered if you knew that the population tested was all people between the age of 18 and 25 versus all people between 55 and 70. Your expectations as to the meaning of whatever is being researched would likely be altered merely by the type of individual included in the population subjected to analyses. Similarly, if a study focused on oil companies in the early 1980s versus the mid- to late 1980s, your expectation of how such companies might perform would likely differ. Alternatively, consider savings and loan institutions in the 1980s versus the early 1990s!

The point is that populations can vary by time, by expected interaction effects of such time context with the variable under study, and by innumerable traits associated with such considerations as geography, industry, age, size, and culture. Would your expectations differ if you knew that only companies listed on the American Stock Exchange were being considered in the analysis, versus another investigation of only private companies? The answer is undoubtedly yes.

FILTERING EFFECTS

Often, researchers begin with an interesting population but are forced, for a variety of reasons, to filter that population before sampling. For example, companies may only be of interest if they have a fiscal year-end in December or if they are nonfinancial entities. Such filtering may be deemed necessary to avoid seasonal or industry effects on the comparability of certain financial measures and ratios among companies sampled.

Similarly, an experiment may require that subjects not have certain types of experience or training, and this requirement may eliminate certain classes of subjects that could have systematically influenced the nature of the findings. Often filters are attempts to control for contaminants to the experimental process, but, in and of themselves, they can contaminate the representativeness of the subsequent analysis.

Good research practice is to report the population of interest, with profile statistics describing that population and then explaining the effects of filtering, including descriptive statistics and verbal descriptions of what is filtered out and what is left. This permits the consumers of the research to draw their own conclusions as to the likely effect of the population filtering on the research process and the results obtained.

RANDOM SELECTION

A desirable attribute of sample selection is randomness. This concept implies that every member of the population has an equal chance of selection. The population is often assigned some type of numbering scheme, and then a *random number generator* is used to select particular sample units. A random number generator is a computer that mathematically ensures that there are no patterns in the sampling units selected. For example, a list of companies on the New York Stock Exchange could be drawn up, numbered sequentially, and then matched to random numbers to determine which companies are to be analyzed. While the random selection does provide substantial comfort that the sample will be *representative* of the underlying population, the degree to which the sample is representative of the entities of interest will depend on the representativeness of the population.

Other forms of random selection besides random number generators are available, but at times they can introduce unintended patterns. As an example, a list of New York Stock Exchange companies might be selected by using a *systematic-sampling approach*, which means selecting every *n*th item. This means that once a single item is selected, the other items within *n* units of that selection do not have a chance of being subsequently chosen. If the population happens to have some order that is tied to the conclusion one wishes to draw, then that pattern might emerge in the sample to distort the conclusions drawn. This could arise due to ordering by industry type, size, or some similar attribute of the company, including alphabetical ordering. As long as the order of the population has no relevance to the research question, the systematic sampling approach should result in a representative sample for evaluation.

The term *haphazard sampling* has been applied to an attempt to select a random sample without using a formal random selection method. For example, if you wished to sample people from a crowd and just walked aimlessly, selecting subjects haphazardly, the claim would be made that this judgmental selection was intended to produce similar results to those obtainable from using random number generators. However, people may have certain taste effects that result in unintended patterns. For example, individuals may tend to choose subjects of similar height or of similar age with a frequency that is not representative of the population. For this reason, haphazard sampling cannot be used as a basis for statistically valid inferences, as would be the case if random number sampling is used. Yet, it is common to draw analogies between haphazard sampling and random selection approaches.

DIRECTED SAMPLING

As an alternative to a random sample, some studies will purposefully select unrepresentative groups on which to perform a study. For example, researchers in the sciences purposefully seek out people with various colds or afflictions in order to determine if some treatment has the intended effect. By a similar token, a matched control sample will be driven by the characteristics of the treatment sample. As explained earlier, the matching process precludes consideration of variables that are used to match the control group and treatment group.

Some researchers will design the study to maximize the "affected" groups of interest to a study on the premise that, if an effect is not discernible for that group, then it is unlikely it would be found in a random sample or be of importance in drawing inferences to a wider group. As an example, bankrupt firms might be elected for study, in lieu of companies that are financially troubled, on the premise that the failed firms would be more likely to have resorted to various mechanisms to buy time such as a change in accounting principles. If the effect were observable for the bankrupt companies, future research could investigate whether the results also held for financially troubled companies or other groups of interest.

Directed sampling assumes that the researcher has accepted an inability to draw inferences to the general population and, instead, has redefined the population of interest in a narrower sense for testing purposes. The price of directing the study is that the inferences drawn must be similarly directed to the population from which the sample was selected.

SAMPLE SIZE

Beyond the selection of the sample, a critical consideration is the sample size. Formulas and tables, well conceived in mathematical theory and tradition, are available for the determination of *sample size*. However, each of these computations requires the researcher to make some judgments about the purpose of the sample, the nature of conclusions to be drawn, the level of reliability and accuracy desired, and the nature of the population in terms of tolerable and expected error rates, if that is the nature of what is under study. In other words, separate criteria apply depending on whether a researcher wishes to quantify an amount, such as the dollar effect of a change in accounting principle, or merely wishes to assess the frequency with which a change in accounting principle arises. The jargon commonly applied is that the dollar effect would be *variables sampling*, while the incidence of some event is an *attribute sampling* question.

In variables sampling, as well as attributes sampling, the variability of the population of interest is an important determinant of required sample size. The simplest example is to pose the following question: If you had an urn full of marbles, all of the same color, how many marbles would you have to draw to tell what color the marbles are? The clear answer would be one. A sample size of one would be totally sufficient to answer the research question. On the other hand, if the urn had three colors represented, in equal proportions, the sample size necessary to identify the three colors would be substantially more than one. If you keep this example in mind, you will be able to form a reasonable-ness assessment of whether you believe a particular sample is sufficient to capture the variation expected for the population to be tested in a particular research study.

Beyond variability, key determinants of sample size are the desired reliability and accuracy. *Reliability* is also referred to as the *confidence level*, and it quantifies the likelihood of producing similar sample results if repeated samples were taken. *Accuracy* is also referred to as *precision*, and it asks: If you were to use the average value of the sample to estimate the population's average, how close would such an estimate be, at a specified reliability level?

In attributes sampling, another key consideration is how close the *expected error rate* is to what is considered a *tolerable rate*. If much higher incidence of a trait or error is permitted than what is expected, then the sample size should not have to be large to achieve an acceptable point estimate of error. On the other hand, the question is also raised of what precision interval you will accept around such a point estimate, at a given level of confidence. The concept of an interval recognizes that any estimate can be overstated or understated. As long as the approach taken to form an estimate is unbiased, then it is as likely to be one direction off as the other, and precision is applied most often in a two-sided manner to describe the attribute of interest. Of course, if the sole concern is for one direction, as might be the case when the researcher wants to be certain that an error rate is not too high, the interval for precision will often be defined as one-sided and will merely set a ceiling on the error rate, based on the sampling results.

DEMAND THE FULL STORY

You may have noticed the frequency with which announcers of polls will state that some finding has a margin for error of 2 percent. While that information is useful, as it implies the width of the precision interval, it is only part of the information you need in order to evaluate how much reliance you might be willing to place on a sample result. You also need to be given a confidence level. Without some idea of the reliability level provided by the sample result, the precision alone is virtually meaningless. In an attributes sample, three pieces of information are needed: the acceptable average incidence, the precision desired around that average, and the level of confidence desired. If you are interested in the rate of error in a database that has been assembled for analysis, you might state that you wish an error rate to average 2 percent, are willing to permit a precision around that rate of 3 percent, and have set the required reliability at a 95 percent confidence. With these three pieces of information, all individuals would determine the same sample size, given some idea of the size of the population being tested.

IS BIGGER NECESSARILY BETTER?

Researchers who assume that "bigger is better" will presume that a larger sample size is always preferable. While it is the case that larger samples reduce sampling error and enhance the reliability and precision of estimates formulated, a possibility exists that one might produce *statistical significance* in the absence of *practical significance*. In other words, if you take a large enough sample, almost anything is statistically significant due to the extremely tight precision available for drawing inferences.[17] Yet the magnitude of the amount may be of no interest from a practical perspective.

Indeed, some have even argued that smaller samples should be far more persuasive than large samples because if something is found to be of statistical significance it has to be a very substantial effect in order to have the discernible effect noted statistically. In contrast, something of no consequence can be made to appear to be statistically significant merely by enlarging the sample size. Of course, since small-sample artifacts can arise, some balance in sample-size determination is desirable. Consider the proverb "for example is no evidence."

COST-BENEFIT CONSIDERATIONS

Determination of sample size is largely a *cost-benefit choice* in research settings. Larger sample sizes are usually more expensive in every aspect of performing the research and may preclude the depth of study due to the breadth of considerations. However, while sample selection, data collection, administration of the experiment, analysis of the data, and challenges in ensuring similar calibration and observation of evidence created are all likely to increase as sample size grows, benefits do accrue. The likely representativeness of the findings and their statistical significance increase as a function of the sample size, in most settings. Yet, as already suggested, too much of a good thing is possible, to the point where researchers can mislead themselves and focus on statistical significance of little if any practical significance.

OVERVIEW

Sample selection entails population definition, filtering often for pragmatic reasons, choosing the sampling units, and setting the sample size. Each of these steps has implications for the quality of the likely findings and the ability to draw inferences from the sample to unsampled units in the same population. Judgmental inference to other populations is likely to be a function of whether reason exists to suspect that the sample under study is distinct in the manner it behaves or the patterns and associations observed. The astute researcher will consider consumers' desire to draw analogies to various groups and will evaluate the costs and benefits of selecting the sample in a particular manner.

CHAPTER 5

THE ROLE OF ASSUMPTIONS

Progress in science is marked by the production of accurately predictive and ever more nearly "true theories."[18]

Old theory is challenged and replaced by new and more successful theories.[19]

This iterative development of theory often involves invoking assumptions and then gradually relaxing these assumptions as a vehicle for developing richer theories. Assumptions are sometimes viewed as a necessary evil and have prompted a number of jokes due, in some cases, to their perceived absurdity. In particular, a great deal of humor has arisen from the use of assumptions by economists. For example, consider the widespread story of three individuals stranded on an island who discover a can of food and are deliberating on how to open the can. When the economist is asked how to proceed, the inevitable words come forth: "Assume a can opener. . . ." Then there is the oft-quoted approach to the word *assume* which points out that when one assumes, the assumptions may make an "ass" out of "u" and "me." The idea is not too far off base, since the quality of information communicated from research may very well hinge on the assumptions underlying the theoretical and empirical work performed.

THE POSITIVE THEORY DEBATE

One cannot discuss the role of assumptions without first recognizing the key debate in the academic literature as to whether concerns for assumptions are well placed. The so-called positive theory approach, eloquently communicated by Nobel-prize winning economist Milton Friedman,[20] suggests that the critical focus should be on a theory's predictability rather than on its assumptions. The assumptions are viewed as simplifying mechanisms that permit the development of a theoretical framework that formulates predictions, which are then tested. The theory producing the best predictions should be prized, regardless of the lack of realism inherent in the underlying assumption.

In his exposition, Milton Friedman points out that "in a vacuum" is often invoked in scientific theory, and despite the inherent lack of reality in such an assumption, the related theories have been powerful in their predictive performance. He likewise points out that a billiard player's expertise can be effectively described using geometry, but it may be unrealistic to expect that the player himself could describe his plays in such technical theoretical terms. The point, of course, is that the assumption of geometry underlying the effectiveness of various plays does not damage the predictability of which pocket will hold the billiard ball at the end of a given play, even if the player never heard of a single theorem!

Economics, finance, and accounting theories invoke a number of theories in developing testable hypotheses. One common assumption is that individuals have homogeneous expectations—an assumption distinct from reality. This assumption simplifies analytical methods and is often coupled with an assumption such as risk neutrality, despite the clear evidence of a great deal of risk-averse investment activity observable in the real world. While the positive theory approach would look to the results of predictions to test competing theories, others would ask how representative of reality the assumptions are and would challenge a theory not only on the basis of its relative predictive performance, but also on the basis of how closely it is able to approximate reality.[21]

RELAXING ASSUMPTIONS

The focus on assumptions commonly leads to enhancement of theories through the *relaxing of assumptions* and derivation of the effects of such a step toward reality. Implications of a theory may be totally different once heterogeneous expectations are permitted, or once a different attitude toward risk is assumed to exist. Although a perfect mirror of reality is not demanded in theory development by those who pay attention to assumptions, discomfort is experienced when the assumptions are at total odds with what is already known.

ASSUMPTIONS IN SAMPLE SELECTION

As already suggested, some researchers assume that a particular sample will be void of systematic patterns or bias with respect to the research question. They likewise assume that the sample will be representative of target populations in which those consuming the research are likely to have an interest. These assumptions will undercut the quality of the research if they are at odds with common sense. For example, companies whose stocks are traded on the New York Stock Exchange will be expected to exhibit certain types of biases as to size of operations, ownership structure, and corporate governance and regulatory effects that may well interact with the research focus. When this is the case, the findings are not likely to be accepted as necessarily applicable to over-the-counter companies.

SAMPLES AVAILABLE FOR ANALYSIS

In research conducted by mail, the researcher will have available only that sample of subjects who choose to respond. The assumption is made that respondents are similar to *nonrespondents*. Yet, this idea is not intuitively appealing, because respondents are likely to be more affected by or more strongly interested in the topic of the mailed case study or survey since they allocated time to completing the instrument and returning it, whereas nonrespondents presumably discarded the instrument.

A common approach to testing the assumption of similarity of respondents to nonrespondents is a technique known as *wave analysis*. This compares early respondents to late respondents on the premise that the later respondents are more similar to the nonrespondents. If a difference in response emerges between the two groups, then the assumption is challenged. However, if the two groups are found to have virtually equivalent responses, researchers often claim that the assumption that respondents and nonrespondents are reasonably similar is supported.

While providing some indirect evidence regarding the nature of respondents, both early and late, the wave analysis may fail to capture the nonrespondent in any manner. The fact is that late respondents nonetheless choose to answer. In contrast, the nonrespondent continued to ignore the research effort. A well-designed research effort by mail will try to describe the characteristics of the population originally sampled, in tandem with the characteristics of the respondents. Such information will permit the consumer of the research to describe the nonrespondent and to detect systematic patterns in terms of who did and did not choose to participate in the research. For example, it may be observed that no company with fewer than 10,000 employees chose to participate in the study, despite the inclusion of 1,000 such companies in the original population and 10 such companies in the sample. If the research issue has a possible relationship to size of the entity, then a limitation would arise in the ability to draw inferences applicable to smaller entities.

ANALYSIS

Empirical research is commonly analyzed via statistical tools. Various *statistical tests* require that certain underlying assumptions be met. These assumptions usually relate to the type of data being analyzed and the *distribution* or shape of the data. As an example, we have described the distinction between cardinal and ordinal data—the former would be all real numbers, which can be analyzed mathematically and via ratios, and the latter type is a ranking. *Nominal data* may also be used. Such data is a classification or qualitative dimension, often coded as yes or no (1 or 0) or industry code 1 versus 2. Certain statistical tests are designed to address classification data—such as the *Chi-square statistics*—while other tools require ordinal or cardinal data—most *modeling techniques* require such attributes for the majority of the data being analyzed. It is always possible to use techniques that require less stringent assumptions than the ones originally considered (e.g., the use of tests appropriate for a weaker scale of measurement). However, such a practice will tend to throw away information available through use of the more tailored tools.[22]

Statistical tests are classified into two major categories: *parametric statistics* and *nonparametric statistics*. They differ primarily in their assumptions regarding the underlying distribution of the data under analysis. Parametric statistics require *normal distributions*, which are smooth, bell-shaped symmetrical curves, adequately described by the *mean* and *standard deviation* (i.e., average and dispersion measure). In contrast, nonparametric statistics do not assume a particular underlying distribution. They tend to describe relationships through rankings, signs, and *medians* (halfway points), rather than means or similar descriptive traits.

A researcher is expected to select the tool of analysis for which the assumptions are met. Considerations in such choices will include attention to the number of variables; scale of measurement; objective of the analysis; the existence of dependent, as distinct from independent, variable(s); linearity or lack thereof; matching possibilities; standardization; presence of intervening variables; and the relevance of assumptions.[23] Of course, the more obscure the statistical tool selected, in order to meet the characteristics of the underlying data, the more difficult it is at times to communicate the research results to those who are interested. As a consequence, some researchers contend that no practically significant differences arise between results obtained using the theoretically preferred tool and those resulting from the more common statistical tool (despite the fact that the underlying assumptions of that tool are met).[24] Indeed, a rather large body of literature exists that describes how resilient or robust particular statistical tools are to relaxing particular assumptions.

Advisable practice is to concurrently disclose the results for the theoretically preferred tool and for the one most familiar to those consuming the research, assuming the two produce similar results. However, as the results move apart, the researcher should always opt for the theoretically appropriate tool, since it may well be the problem of underlying assumptions that is creating a misleading result.

THE CONCEPT OF HOLD-OUT SAMPLES

When research involves the formulation of an empirical model, an assumption implicitly made is that the results of such a model would hold for other samples from the same population. Yet, it is possible to compute findings that are peculiar to the particular sample under study and would fail to be applicable to other sampling units. To guard against such a possibility, a researcher will strive to collect a *hold-out sample*—an independent set of sampling units for which predictions are formulated from the model and tested as to their applicability. If a model fails to perform well for the hold-out sample, two possibilities exist: (1) the model is sample-specific and needs to be generalized to avoid its peculiar fit to the sample on which it was based or (2) the hold-out sample is not representative of the population from which it was drawn. A second hold-out sample drawn independently of the first could test the likelihood of the second possibility, which is typically low if selected in a random manner.

Since data are expensive to collect, hold-out samples are often viewed as a luxury. In such a setting, the threat of a nonrepresentative or sample-specific finding persists. An increasingly common approach to the dilemma is to test the resiliency of the model to varying the sampling units on which the model is based. For example, random selections from the sampling units could be made and models reestimated and tested for their equivalence to the formulated model.[25] Presumably, if a peculiar trait of certain observations resulted in a *statistical artifact*, this would show up through such tests of model stability.

The consumer of research in which no hold-out sample is tested and model stability is not reviewed in a systematic manner should be wary of the possibility of sample-specific findings. In addition, consumers should understand that the results of modeling without a separate independent test on a hold-out sample will always appear to be stronger than they would likely be in a predictive mode. In other words, a given *sample's descriptive power* is commonly greater than its *predictive power*.

MODEL SPECIFICATION

The assumption applicable to many model specifications is that no omitted variables pose a problem in either interpreting or applying that model. Possible *uncontrolled factors* in models of companies' economic activities include industry classification, size, capital structure, corporate governance, regulated status, and the time period in which the evaluation is being performed. While it is never possible to test all potential variables for their relationship to a given model, the theoretical framework for the inquiry is expected to suggest variables that need to be controlled. Rather than to assume away the effect of such variables, their inclusion in the model facilitates testing of such an assumption as a routine step in the *model-building process*.

The research process has been described as one of abstraction, modeling, comparison of predictions to empirics, and revision.[26] Such a process often entails iterative modeling.

ASSUMPTIONS IN COMMUNICATION

Once the researcher has carefully evaluated the assumptions (applicable to sample selection and later analyses and subject to testing in the modeling phase of the research) necessary to the theoretical framework, the question arises of how to effectively communicate the role of assumptions. *Full disclosure* is preferable, with a discussion of the researcher's expectations as to the likely implications of relaxing those assumptions applicable to the research project. If certain assumptions have not been supported, this should be stated, and the possible ill effects of such assumptions should be disclosed. Some assumptions, if not met, mean that the results are better than reported, while others create the impression of better findings than actually exist. The latter effect is

particularly dangerous to those planning on using the results in some decision framework. Hence, a bold warning that the results are not as good as they appear is essential
in the communication process.

Some assumptions may be an inherent facet of a certain methodology. It is rather
common to have joint tests of hypotheses, where the results depend on the assumption
that the model being used is valid. When a joint test applies to a particular research
setting, that fact needs to be spelled out clearly. This ensures that the reader of the
research results will appreciate the contingent nature of the findings.

OVERVIEW

Assumptions play a role in the initial theoretical development, in the sample selection
and analysis, and in communicating the results of research. While they are commonly
required to simplify both theoretical and empirical inquiry, their correspondence to
reality or lack thereof tends to be of interest to those drawing inferences and those
thinking about applying the results of the research effort. Importantly, enhancement of
past research is often accomplished by relaxing assumptions that have been imposed on
earlier work. At times, this process leads to important improvements of our understanding of various phenomena.

CHAPTER 6

COMMUNICATION

There is never certainty in science, and the weight of evidence for or against a hypothesis can never be assessed completely objectively.[27]

In light of the quote above, care in communication is particularly important. Bias should be avoided and caveats should be clearly set forth. Jargon should be minimized to enhance effective communication.

The *Doctor Fox story* is the epitome of what is often the Achilles' heel of research—the proliferation of "jargonese." The story is based on a real research study directed at demonstrating one reason why jargonese is so dominant. In the research, an actor was hired to pose as a visiting expert who was to make a presentation before a group of psychologists and psychiatrists. The speech that was full of nonsense and loaded with "jargonese" had been drafted. The actor dutifully learned his lines, was introduced as the eminent Dr. Fox, and proceeded to deliver the speech. His speech was applauded and praised with evaluations of "most impressive" and "clear and stimulating." It would seem that the proliferation of jargon, even though nonsensical in content, had impressed the audience. The findings of the study supported the so-called Doctor Fox hypothesis that researchers cling to jargon because of its role in upgrading the impression made on consumers, even if consumers have no understanding of the substance of what is being communicated.[28]

The real implications of the Doctor Fox story would seem to be that dangers arise from the use of jargon. Those dangers include the fact that work can be accorded praise that is unmerited and obtained purely due to the impression created by the use of technical terminology. Moreover, jargon serves as a barrier to real understanding. It should not be expected of consumers of research that they know the technical terminology that is routinely used by the researcher. While many argue that parsimonious communication vehicles among researchers require jargon, the fact remains that research needs to withstand the scrutiny of third parties who are not necessarily involved in that particular line of research. In addition, greater synergy among lines of inquiry and different disciplines can only arise from a sharing of ideas and findings. Such sharing is virtually precluded if each group excessively uses esoteric jargon.

BE WARY OF JARGONESE

Just as the Dr. Fox audience should not have been taken in by the technical-sounding discourse of the actor, you should be particularly wary when a research study is inaccessible to anyone other than the specialist. An attempt should be made by the researcher to translate the general research question, the nature of related theory, the empirical execution or analytical approach, and the implications in tandem with caveats, limitations, and open questions tied to various assumptions invoked along the way. Without such translation, the results are virtually unusable and suffer from the possibility of acceptance through ignorance rather than through rigorous scrutiny.

A CHECKLIST FOR COMPLETENESS OF DISCLOSURE

An invisible checklist should be apparent in the manner in which research is communicated. Each stage of the scientific process should be apparent, with disclosures of assumptions invoked, biases tested, problems identified, steps taken to contain such problems, and results obtained. Tests of assumptions should be reported or caveats noted as to which assumptions may not hold and how they are expected to potentially influence the findings or approach taken in the research. Each of the concerns for internal and external validity, detailed in earlier chapters, should be addressed in the design and communication of the research project and findings. In particular, concerns as to whether the findings are likely to be applicable to other populations should be expressed.

DUE CARE

Care in exposition, or the lack thereof, will often be a telltale sign of the likely care exercised in the research process. For example, a quasi-experimental approach should state the association among variables of interest without implying a causal linkage. By the same token, if certain assumptions of a statistical technique are not met or have not been tested to ensure they are met, such facts should be clearly stated rather than buried as problems detectable only through careful scrutiny of the reader and perhaps not even then.

VISIONARY STRENGTHS

The researcher is likely to be in the best position to share visionary insights as to the direction of *future research*. Visions as to what the next step will be in this line of inquiry and how it might answer the unanswered questions raised by the current study are to be communicated to facilitate the taking of such a step. If a researcher lacks vision as to where his or her project fits in the pursuit of knowledge, then the research contribution, if any, is far more likely to be obscure. A visionary strength in the communication of research holds much promise for long-term contribution of the study at hand.

CAVEATS

While many joke that the concept of labeling microwave ovens as not being useful to dry the fur or coats of various living creatures is ridiculous and is a sign of how excessive disclosure practices have become, the benefits of effective labeling cannot be denied. The labeling of financial information as unaudited establishes certain expectations likely to be different from information labeled ''audited.'' By a similar token, labels belong on research studies that explain the likely credibility of various aspects of the work. These caveats will relate to known limitations and assumptions applicable to each stage of the scientific process that are expected to influence either internal or external validity.

By describing the nature of the researcher's concerns, as well as reasons why the researcher may or may not expect the findings to hinge on such concerns, the researcher permits the consumers of the study to draw their own conclusions. The researcher's perspective is valuable, but the various users of the research may note that various aspects of the research have different implications for their intended use.

For example, consider the research related to bankruptcy prediction that produced what was referred to earlier as a Z-score, intended to assess the likelihood of failure. The performance of the Z-score in terms of identifying companies that later went bankrupt was reported to be promising and sparked use of the Z-score algorithm by investors. Certain auditing firms also considered using the Z-score for the purposes of assessing the likelihood of a client company being a going concern. The problem arose that the Z-score indicated that a number of companies that did not eventually go bankrupt were nonetheless ''expected'' to fail according to the bankruptcy modeling approach. The investor had not been particularly concerned over these apparent false signals, since little cost resulted from precluding investment in certain companies given the wide assortment of available investment prospects that were considered reasonable substitutes. In stark contrast, the auditors had clients with whom they were affiliated and with whom they were likely to maintain a long-term relationship. To dispose of a client merely because a Z-score flagged financial difficulty was impractical, given the high number of false signals observed. Disclosure of going-concern risks due merely to the Z-score was similarly viewed to be unreasonable, since false signals were so common. Hence, a tool applauded as useful for the investor did not offer the same advantages to the auditor. Numerous other examples could be crafted to illustrate the point that research findings are unlikely to have homogeneous implications for all readers, including the caveats associated with such research findings.

TRICKS OF THE TRADE

As a consumer of a substantial number of research studies that are likely to be plagued by the Dr. Fox syndrome and are too often specialist by nature, you will need to keep in mind certain tricks of the trade in consuming technical research reports. Begin with a perusal of the reference section, since the referenced literature commonly suggests where the research is expected to fit and to what subject matter it relates. Moreover, the quality of the work from a timeliness point of view and its originality or uniqueness can begin to be inferred based on your familiarity with the literature cited.

The *footnotes* are an invaluable source of caveats, limitations, assumptions, and points that have been raised by peers as potentially relevant and probably not treated in a complete manner by the research design. A perusal of the footnotes will sometimes suggest that the rest of the paper is not worthy of any additional investment of time. This can result from the caveats being so pervasive in their influence on the particular decision setting in which you have an interest that the research loses its apparent relevance to you as a reader.

Most journals require an *abstract*, introduction, and conclusion. These are usually written to facilitate effective key-word searches by various literary databases and are intended to communicate in reasonably accessible terminology the objective, methodology, and findings of the research. If these passages are unreadable, then there is little hope for effective communication being an attribute of the rest of the paper.

Appendices are often created for technical details and analytical proofs, again as a simplifying tool to make the research itself more comprehensible. The existence of such appendices makes avoidance of the Dr. Fox scenario much more probable.

As the literature in a field advances, a norm is to cite foundational work rather than repeating the theory and methodological details already well explained in past literature. Make a point to pull copies of such cited work for reference as you work through a research report that has built on such past lines of inquiry. Frustration can easily build up without access to explanations of the foundation on which a piece of research is based. Yet it is unreasonable to expect valuable journal space in any field to be redundant over time. The sole responsibility of the journal and author is to point the interested reader in the direction where "full disclosure" can be obtained.

Finally, if a perverse finding or interpretation is made in your reading of a research report, or if an apparent contradiction appears in the research, do not hesitate to contact the author of the research report directly. Every researcher appreciates a third party reading his or her research, and errors do arise in the communication and the publishing process. You can spin your wheels far longer than necessary due to a hesitancy to go "straight to the horse's mouth." Yet the more information you absorb, the more you will grow to appreciate how relatively common errors are in research publications. Despite the authors', editor's, reviewers', and proofreaders' efforts, errors will slip through and show up in the final published text. By accessing the author's knowledge directly, not only will you avoid pondering an erroneous finding or inference, you will also be able to obtain clarification as to why some item thought to be an error or misleading is indeed appropriate. An added benefit will accrue to the researcher—the next time that individual reports on related research, the source of the problem in communication can be addressed to avoid such questions arising in other readers' minds. The researcher will no doubt be appreciative.

OVERVIEW

The communication process is fraught with problems associated with the technical nature of the material being communicated, the unfortunate attraction of complexity as a means of making favorable impressions, and the limitation of journal space. Nonetheless, full disclosure can be expected either through footnotes or citations to related literature. If research is inaccessible or not communicated in tandem with caveats and future research expectations, then its relative contribution is likely to be small. In contrast, full disclosure will permit readers to evaluate the research contributions for their personal needs and the expected context in which the research findings are to be applied. An effective researcher will keep in mind the heterogeneous nature of the readership when communicating results and will translate technical notions and use appendices and similar vehicles to improve the communication of approaches and results across disciplines and to diverse interested parties.

CHAPTER 7

"THE FISHING HOLE"

The hardest crossword puzzle to solve is the one in which we have penciled in a wrong word and are too stubborn or fixated to erase it; in much the same way, it is often easier to solve a problem when you are merely ignorant than when you are wrong.

—*Sidney J. Harris*[29]

Researchers must be open-minded to ensure recognition of wrong conclusions. Otherwise, they may spin their wheels endlessly, striving to corroborate an erroneous conclusion. In reading certain research reports, attempting to cling to mistakes such as claimed causal factors, and offering various explanations and interpretations, you will, at times, be reminded of stories about the old fishing hole. Oh, yes, there was Buddy's tale of woe as to why he failed to catch any fish one crisp autumn day: Leaves had fallen into the water. He was thinking about suing the owners of those trees, as he knew he'd lost at least a dozen fish that Saturday.

Those of us who knew Buddy had to smirk at least a little. We all knew that Buddy fished every Saturday and had his on and off days. The fact is, he liked to scrimp on bait, had an old fishing rod, and shared the fishing hole with at least a half dozen neighbors, several of whom were crackerjack sportspeople. Somehow, the leaves hadn't stopped everybody else's line from getting a bite.

When Buddy had bent everyone's ear in the coffee shop, a few telling questions were posed: "What was your excuse last week, Buddy?" "Why wasn't Kevin's fishing affected?" "It might help if you invested in a new rod; you know, technology's moved along in the last decade!" "You have to entice the critters. Where was your bait?" "Maybe the competition's just too tough!"

Of course, Buddy always had an answer. "Last week, I didn't have the right bait." "Kevin was just lucky (never mind that he had fancy flies); besides, he gets preferential treatment at the bait shop." "Anyway, everyone knows what tall tales Kevin tells." "What's more, I don't need a new fishing rod; the one I have has served me well for a decade and will do so for another ten years, no doubt." "I do use bait; I'm just not wasteful or extravagant like the others." "I'm not outclassed; why, I've pulled more catfish out of that hole than anyone, if you add up the number of catches for just the peak season—though I know others are after different fish." "I'm convinced that if I can hook catfish, it's inevitable that I'll catch the others."

50

Just as Buddy's claims sounded "fishy" to the townsfolk, characterizations of causal factors, the evidence offered in support of such claimed causes, and the denial of the relevance of the facts of the situation will no doubt remind you of Buddy at the fishing hole. Consider the following explanations.

"I MUST HAVE LOST AT LEAST A HUNDRED FISH."

To estimate the effect of various causal factors, simulations are sometimes used. Just as the fish don't bite upon request, no reason exists for a simulated result to necessarily reflect reality. Too often, the assertions that certain results would be produced in accordance with a model sounds a lot like counting your fish before they're hooked.

We'd expect those using a simulation to evaluate the merits of the underlying assumptions relative to competing assumptions, much as a sponsor of a fishing contest would evaluate Buddy against his competition. Yet, too often researchers offer no insights as to the competing assumptions under consideration, the rates of rejection of such assumptions, or a reason to expect that the assumptions invoked are typical.

"THE LEAVES ARE RESPONSIBLE."

The cause of the model's results automatically produces certain estimates. Never mind that these estimates may not correspond to evidence of what happens in the real world! Ignore the fact that the evidence didn't support a simulation's expectations! If only those leaves hadn't fallen. . . .

"I DIDN'T CATCH ANY FISH, SO THAT PROVES THE LEAVES ARE THE CULPRIT."

The evidence offered in support of some models is that a particular event is observable. Yet, the questions posed to Buddy are similarly relevant to a researcher.

- There are occasions on which such events are observed and claimed results are not observed, so why would the claimed causal event on this particular occasion necessarily be expected to initiate the predicted result?
- Why have similar results to those predicted been observed in different settings without the causal event?
- What other causal factors have been considered?
- If a claimed causal factor had the predicted result, might the environment be altered in some manner, so that other causal factors are triggered?

Too often,the nature of the evidence researchers cite is not that of an objective analysis of historical data using statistical tools to formulate an estimate. Instead, the model is simply a simulation of what would have happened if one assumes that some event occurred. Of course, if that event looks unreasonable, then its effects might be portrayed in some manner that makes it appear more palatable. The simulation often proceeds by invoking assumption upon assumption. Since simulations are nothing but make-believe scenarios in which results are generated by prespecified rules and relationships that have no necessary connection to the real world, fiction can result.

The scenario often does not stop at one assumption, but compounds one effect onto another. In this compounding process, it is easy to ignore the real-world existence of evidence contrary to both underlying assumptions and their assumed effect.

The evidence offered in support of various dimensions of the model can be likened to Buddy's ready answers to the coffee shop crew. Contentions that hypothesized results differ from observed results because some causal factor was not controlled is the epitome of biased inquiry. Be skeptical of the researcher who asserts whenever results are other than expected that such discrepancy is due to a methodological problem. Similarly, be wary of those accusing others of misreporting and always assuming that others told taller tales or otherwise mischaracterized some aspect of their research. Likewise, watch for dismissed control variables that are termed unnecessary. Why others see benefits to such control variables is too often left unexplained. Watch for analogies that don't quite work, because researchers make generalizations—just like Buddy's claim of what should be true since he could catch catfish. Never mind that one ability may be quite different from another ability. In the same way as catching fish besides catfish was not "inevitable" for Buddy, one effect in one context by no means demonstrates the inevitable effect elsewhere.

In identifying evidence for presentation, a researcher may sound a good deal like Buddy, cautioning that measurement of his or her findings' performance must be over some carefully defined period. Benchmarks seem to be moving targets that must meet precise criteria in order to represent the "right" measurement stick. Don't be concerned that the movements in the target are often in opposite directions! In particular, too short or too long a period of analysis may produce the "wrong" results. Patterns that appear erratic are due to noise, but those in the expected direction are discernible trends that are cited as clearly demonstrating important points! (This is tongue in cheek, of course.)

Longitudinal analyses are fine to demonstrate certain items, yet it is claimed they are irrelevant to all other tests of the models at hand. Cross-sectional comparisons are advocated, but one must take care to understand when averages are relevant, when other comparison groups are more appropriate, and what is not comparable. One should not be surprised when it is pointed out that some uncontrolled factor, not thought necessary within the simulation itself, is nonetheless of such significant import to preclude an effective comparison of apparent relevance.

"YOU CAN'T COMPARE ME TO KEVIN; WHY, HE HAS . . ."

No comparison on factual analysis appears to have relevance to some researchers. They dismiss as immaterial statistical regression models' failure to meet generally accepted standards of model building, such as the testing of the basic underlying assumptions of the tool. That aside, the fact that the interpretation of the models is inconsistent with what is claimed to be past patterns is somehow irrelevant. Indeed, if that is not enough, consider the tendency to term a variety of observed events as being irrelevant (though often even definitionally illogical).

Movement in variables not controlled for in a particular research study is claimed to have no bearing on the likelihood of the actual results comparing to model expectations.

As correlation evidence is reported that indicates an unexpected inverse relationship, some researchers will attempt to attribute that association to mathematical similarities in how some third factor (often unspecified) affects the items of primary interest. Yet, that same researcher has no difficulty asserting a causal linkage when the variables are correlated positively, as expected despite the similar underlying issue of the extent to which some third variable might drive the results. One is asked to ignore the fact that a first-differencing model is essential to address the question of interest and that the positive correlation identified was inevitable, given the joint effects of some controlled influence and autocorrelation (a problem prevalent in longitudinal time-series regression analyses).

The facts that in recent years, as one variable has increased, such as time spent fishing, another has not consistently been increased are asserted to be caused by other factors. Yet, the reasonableness of the overall data set may well have been called into question, which would have undermined most related computations in a simulation had discrepancies been objectively explored.

If other actions are needed to have a given effect, too many researchers see no need to alter a model. This is despite the presence of a theory; for some reason, it doesn't apply to the case at hand or sample under study, or so you are made to believe.

Overall analyses by a researcher should be compared to knowledge already possessed, and differences should be investigated. Comparability to similar samples under study is appropriate. Their exposure to misreporting or real differences should be explored. Despite research findings, little can be inferred without considering each of these sources of corroborating or conflicting evidence.

"NOW THIS IS NOT A TALL TALE."

Certain telltale signs give away fish stories, and some of the signs pervade research reports. Although anyone trained in research design knows the difference in demonstrating association versus causality, some will use terms such as *proves* or *demonstrates* in describing how statistical analyses tie to various causal assertions. No such tie can be appropriately drawn. Similarly, a researcher tests assumptions and models for reasonableness. The attitude that too often persists in research reports is that no comparison works; either it is irrelevant because it cannot capture the hypothetical what-if analysis asserted to apply, or the differences observed are dismissed as immaterial or artifacts.

In testing a theory, it is essential to design comprehensive, consistent *criteria for evaluation*. As an example, if a relevant criterion is performance relative to some average, then each step of the analysis should make this comparison as a reasonableness check. If the relevant comparison is to some analogous group, then that group should be revisited, in relative terms, each step of the way. In making arguments for comparisons that are irrelevant and relevant, the criteria must be consistent.

Buddy and researchers may appear to have a great deal in common. The spirit of the research may not be consistent with the application of the scientific method or careful consideration of conclusions drawn. Rather, it may take the form of a quilt that accepts patches of evidence consistent with the story and discards whatever evidence is inconsistent. Such a tactic is not a test of a theory or a demonstration of its credibility. Rather, it is an advocacy position with partial information and questionable conclusions.

CHAPTER 8

AN ACCOUNTING SAMPLER

If accounting is important and you change the accounting rules, then the play of the game changes.[30]

The nature of rules, the effects of changes therein, and economic implications are the subject matter of considerable research in accounting. Now that you have considered numerous research design issues and are attuned to common problems to which to be alert, you may well have some curiosity as to the types of research you may encounter. The objective of this chapter is to focus on one area of potential interest and to describe a sample of the major lines of inquiry and the types of findings reported to date. This introduction is intended to whet your appetite to consume various types of research, to appreciate their potential interest, and to also consider the vast spectrum of inquiries across not only economic disciplines, but in every possible area where we seek improved understanding.

WHY CHOOSE ACCOUNTING?

The area of accounting is chosen as the focus of this chapter for several reasons. First, it is a discipline that permeates measurement of economic transactions in all other economic fields. Second, it is a widely misunderstood profession, since individuals often think of green eyeshades and arm bands when the subject of accountants is mentioned. Third, almost every imaginable research technique in the social sciences has been applied to accounting questions. Fourth, the research findings have implications for other fields. Moreover, I often reflect on a question posed to me by a neighbor during my doctoral work in accounting; upon hearing of the subject matter of my graduate work, the neighbor posed the question of what one could possibly be studying at the doctoral level in accounting. Did that mean that I could use a 10-key adding machine far faster than others? While not quite so direct, similar questions of curiosity as to the nature of research in accounting have been posed to me over the years by numerous individuals with whom I have come in contact. Perhaps this chapter will begin to sensitize individuals to the diverse set of interests with which accounting researchers grapple, as well as the potential use of related findings to many walks of life.

MARKET FORCES

As with all business endeavors, markets assume a central role in furthering understanding in accounting. Presumably, the very existence of accounting is a function of demand and supply for information and attestation services (such as the audit process). The questions explored in market-related research often rely on basic economic and finance research. The notion of efficient markets has clear implications for accounting. *Efficient-markets* evidence suggests that markets are able to assimilate information rapidly and to adjust prices in a manner that reflects the future cash flows expected to be generated from a particular investment. Technology has been developed to assess *information content* of a particular news release or financial report. Basically, expected returns are estimated by assuming a continuing relationship between particular companies' returns and that of the market. Then, deviations between expected return and actual return are referred to as *abnormal returns* (or *prediction errors*) and, if statistically significant, are thought to reflect some information content to the particular *event* or release on the day the market reaction is observed.[31]

Information Content

This type of research has drawn various tentative conclusions. Earnings per share are observed to have information content, although numerous competing sources of information also exist that cause fairly sophisticated expectations of later financial announcements. Industries vary in their reaction to news announcements, and this variation is thought to be due to differential levels of noise in the accounting system and the nature of information that is applicable to a particular type of company. Trade tends to increase in volume when information is made available. Market prices tend to reflect qualifications in auditors' reports, as well as the nature of accounting practices. Accounting information correlates to market measures of risk, events such as bankruptcy, and overall market returns. Finally, the market, by and large, appears able to reflect information in footnotes, similar to its ability to impound information from the face of financial statements.

Valuation

A growing line of inquiry concerns the manner in which the market values *derivative securities*, such as stock options, and the implications of such pricing for accounting valuation. Questions of how new financial instruments or economic transactions influence shareholder wealth and bondholders' interests are being addressed, using various market-based tools of analysis. Global markets have raised questions of whether markets are able to account for different accounting systems and tax practices in reaching comparable valuations in various stock exchanges. How global markets have been, are likely to be, or should be regulated—particularly as these questions involve accounting disclosure issues—begs for an answer.

Information Transfer

A similar question that has recently emerged focuses on the notion of *information transfer*, which implies that if a certain company releases information, it is likely to have spillover effects on other companies in the same industry or other facets of the economy that are affected by similar environmental factors. This issue is particularly interesting because it could assist in explaining both the content and timing of information releases. Moreover, as technology increasingly facilitates on-line access to databases, thus replacing reliance on aggregated hard-copy reports on companies' operations, determining what is rightfully proprietary information and what should be a part of full-disclosure requirements will be a challenge. A better understanding of the behavior of information transfer could assist in resolving such regulatory questions.

Quality of Earnings

An added dimension of the market research area concerns the *quality of earnings* issue and whether the market is able to discern the varied noise levels in companies' information systems and financial reporting releases. For example, if management is particularly aggressive in selecting from among accounting choices in a manner that has a tendency to increase reported income, does the market appreciate the effect of such *earnings management* when comparing and contrasting information releases from various companies? Past research has suggested that companies that later fall into financial difficulty, such as the Charter Company,[32] have often used accounting choices as a vehicle to make their reported income appear higher than normal operations might have otherwise been able to achieve. The question as to why companies use earnings management if the market is relatively efficient has to be posed. One tentative reply is that such practices can have real effects avoiding loan covenants (restrictions by lenders); increasing compensation; and decreasing various costs associated with information generation and reporting.

In gaining an understanding of cross-sectional variation in accounting and financial practices among companies, attention has been directed to taxes and bankruptcy costs, managerial signalling, and key personality traits. Research has focused on discretionary disclosure and auditing practices, as well as on the selection of accounting procedures. In addition, mandated accounting changes have been studied, as have companies' reactions to proposed standards. The incidence of voting and lobbying activities (e.g., with the Financial Accounting Standards Board or Capitol Hill), positions taken, and influences on financing, production, and investment decisions of compulsory accounting changes are all being explored.

As depicted in Figure 4, research has a potentially pervasive influence on standard setting in the accounting arena. Research can explore the credibility of parties' assertions (such as bias toward overstatement of income by managers of troubled companies) and can thereby influence perceptions. Consequences of

FIGURE 4
Role of Research for Standard Setting

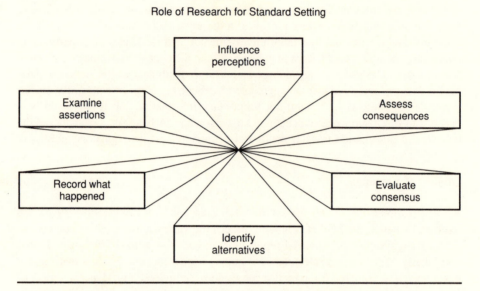

Role of Research for Standard Setting

Adapted from Paul A. Griffin, *Research Report: Usefulness to Investors and Creditors of Information Provided by Financial Reporting*, 2nd ed. (Stamford, Conn.: Financial Accounting Standards Board, 1987), p. 25.

proposed regulation can be assessed, as can the effects of rules already implemented. Through research, alternatives can be identified, and the degree of consensus as to the feasibility of, preferability of, and actual experience with such choices can be measured.

Enhancements

The market-based research has emphasized public companies on major stock exchanges, has focused on aggregate decision results as reflected in rational expectations of market participants, and has gradually focused on improved information as to when something has occurred and whether particular trades are observed, even within a given minute of the day. Improved technology has facilitated regulatory monitoring of insider trading and other market activities. Future inquiries will no doubt strive to expand attention beyond the major U.S. exchanges and will blend both improved information sources and research technology to hopefully explain a greater proportion of market reactions and patterns relative to accounting information, as well as nonfinancial information generated from companies' databases and other sources.

THE INDIVIDUAL DECISION MAKERS

The focus on aggregate decision making as reflected in market research invariably raises the possibility of segmented markets and a need to consider the individuals comprising the market. Questions have arisen as to whether there are informed and uninformed investors that influence the market in a manner that suggests a need to disaggregate markets into decision makers. This leads to numerous questions of whether decision makers are rational, how they use information, whether particular types of accounting and other information are more useful than others, and whether it is possible to improve decision making through various decision aids, constructive feedback, or such tools as expert systems and artificial intelligence.

Heuristics

To date, we have learned a number of things about the way in which individuals make decisions. Rarely do they perform analysis in a manner that follows either classical probability theory or *Bayesian decision theory* (whereby subjective probabilities are systematically combined with additional evidence to reach a conclusion). People tend to be relatively insensitive to the prior probability of outcomes, sample size, and predictability. Moreover, they have misconceptions of chance and tend to have illusions regarding validity, such as having excessive confidence in some perception due to a good fit with some predicted outcome.[33] Sets of heuristics are used in decision making, leading to errors, biases, and inconsistencies.[34] For example, the manner in which a problem is formulated can affect the initial value at which one begins to analyze a problem and, since insufficient adjustment is common, different results can arise due to this so-called *anchoring and adjustment* problem.[35] The ordering of information is seen, at times, to have a so-called *recency effect*, whereby the more recent information has a greater effect than does older information. By a similar token, some decision makers have a tendency to seek out *confirming evidence* that reinforces their current line of thinking and to downplay, if not discard, *disconfirming evidence*. The advantage of systematic inquiries that identify possible tendencies and quantify their effect is that decision makers can be alerted to their possible shortcomings and work to avoid such pitfalls.

Group Decision Making

While individuals' cognitive processes are being explored, increased attention is being directed to the effect of group and interactive decision making, as well as organizational structure effects, including the role of feedback, self-justification, and performance evaluation of decisions. Do incentive structures alter decisions; what is the influence of computational tools when used by the decision maker?[36] Individuals' experience, the context in which a particular type of task is performed, and the process of analysis are all relevant to how decisions seem to proceed.

The Role of Consensus

A key controversy in behavioral types of research concerns the role of *consensus* and whether this is a desirable attribute and how it relates to accuracy. Assume that accountants do not tend to agree on materiality levels when reporting on a particular company. Is it the case that the number to which all of the accountants will eventually agree is necessarily superior? How important is the communication process in ensuring that the most accurate result emerges?

Research to date suggests high consistency but relatively low consensus among auditors. Decision processes vary substantially among individuals.[37]

Choice

In evaluating alternatives such as accounting choices or implications of investments for accounting numbers, to what extent do decision makers approach the questions as *compensatory models* or *noncompensatory models*? The former permits one aspect to compensate for another, while the latter might set a sort of minimum requirement that would have to be met by all attributes to qualify for consideration. A widely discussed choice in university settings is whether students with work experience, graduate admission test scores, and grade points among the attributes considered for admission should be permitted to have one of these criteria offset another or whether they should be forced to reach at least some minimum floor for each criterion.

THE ELEGANCE OF MODELING

Since so many attributes may well influence decision making, some researchers have sought analytical approaches to clarifying the problem by forcing structure in the form of mathematics and modeling. The models often involve two parties in a one-period world, although advancements have been made in considering more parties and longer time frames to permit the concepts of attestation and reputation to be considered. To illustrate the interesting sorts of findings that can emerge from analytical analyses, consider how one can construct a model in which less information is preferred to more information. Indeed, not only is the person better off knowing less, but that individual will even pay someone to know less. The manner in which this rather nonintuitive result can be made to go away is to introduce some sort of contracting that, for example, involves the sharing of information or commitments to always make a particular selection, thereby eliminating certain concerns that arise from *asymmetrical information* (i.e., being on other than a level playing field because one party has more information than another).

Controllability Concept

A similar analytical structure to which much attention has been directed recently involves the *controllability concept*. The results to date suggest that in order for a performance measure to be of use in evaluating managerial actions, that measure must be influenced by what the manager does.[38] The question posed to other researchers is what the influence is on the conditional probability of the variance of a particular proposed incentive measure, given everything else that we know. Since many performance plans are based on accounting measures, the conditional controllability question promises to guide many future inquiries using a variety of empirical tools. However, one difficulty is that the trait of interest, the extent to which managers' actions influence particular measures, is difficult to observe.

Communication

The elegance of a model is that it can succinctly communicate essential elements that affect some phenomenon or decision. The problem is that it will do so at the expense of some realism. One interesting perspective is that the use of analytics can help to not only clarify problems and elucidate upon ideas, but in addition, to identify unsolvable problems. The advantage of such identification is that the decision maker can quickly turn to decision aids as opposed to searching for an ultimate solution. In such a setting, simulation analysis is a commonly used tool to evaluate the likely effects of some relationship.

MANAGEMENT ACCOUNTING

The manner in which decisions as to what information to gather and use are made by internal accountants and managers, as well as how to analyze such information, is an increasing focal point for researchers. The techniques are often in a *field study* context, whereby an understanding is gained in considerable depth as to how a particular company or groups of companies are handling their accounting system and control process. Problems identified include the lack of timeliness of accounting information; the eroding relevance of certain types of activity bases for allocation of overhead; the difficulty in tracking and integrating qualitative factors into decisions such as capital budgeting decisions; and short-term optimization being at the cost of longer-term competitive needs.

It has been observed that financial accounting needs and associated regulations have at times taken such precedence in the development of information systems within business that the results have been a lack of important information that decision makers need in order to manage operations.

DATABASE MANAGEMENT SYSTEMS (DBMS)

As technology is enhanced, programming capabilities developed, and information retrieval demands increased, demands for research on how to better structure information
systems for control purposes, accessibility, and analysis grow. Researchers have demonstrated that accounting can be viewed as a sort of storytelling function whereby the
economic activities of a company can be viewed as a story's script, the individual
economic participants (such as customers, suppliers, employees, and owners) as its
actors, and the information system itself as the full story. The advantage of such a
perspective is that natural-languages research techniques and rules can be used to
construct accounting "languages." Moreover, certain research projects can begin to
be identified based on commonality of scripts.[39]

In particular, if individuals wished to construct a useful tax-related data base, they
might examine a multitude of court cases, interrelating such cases based on general
scripts rather than merely key words. As one researcher has observed, the scripts of
Romeo and Juliet and *Westside Story* have a similarity of script, although the key-word
search underlying much of the legal research that is currently performed in the tax area
might fail to identify such an overall theme.[40] An opportunity would seem to exist to
construct what are termed *relational databases* that facilitate retrieval of tax court cases
and various precedents that share common overall themes of relevance to decision
makers. These may take the form of information systems with artificial intelligence
extensions that invoke various types of logic to assist a user of such databases.

INTEGRATING RESEARCH AREAS

Many times, the general areas described as fruitful for research overlap and lead to
multimethod explorations. As an example, the mathematical model of rational expectations has numerous implications for how decisions might be made in the marketplace
with respect to pricing, responding to information, and reactions to opportunities for
collusion or use of insider information. *Experimental markets* are being used as a
behavioral tool to study market phenomena using the analytics to formulate predictions
for testing. The experimental-markets approach literally creates a laboratory setting
intended to parallel an operating market. Then, trading rules and instructions are provided and actions are observed and recorded. The process might involve *double auction
bidding* with buyers and sellers, *sealed-bid auctions* to emulate a competitive bidding
type of process, or a multitude of other processes of interest. Individuals' willingness
to give up resources for certain types of information or attestations as to the credibility
of such information has been observed.

The experimental-markets setting has been the basis for conducting simulation-based
research where traders are programmed to behave randomly, as compared to traders
being assumed to apply standard program trading rules. Similarly, through the use of

videotapes, careful attention has been directed toward the way in which information is accessed and used to reach decisions as to how to bid in a market setting.

OVERVIEW

This chapter provides merely a sample of accounting research areas, techniques, tentative findings, and future questions. However, the richness of lines of inquiry should be apparent, as should the need to respect research design trade-offs and various other issues detailed in earlier chapters as we strive to increase our understanding of the world in which we live.

CHAPTER 9

A PROFILE OF A RESEARCHER

Economists' central questions are WHAT, HOW, and FOR WHOM?[41]

In attempting to relate research to practice, it may be useful to describe desired attributes of a researcher and then to try to envision how such a person could help to resolve practice-related issues. With such an objective in mind, I have prepared the following profile:

A researcher must be inquisitive—filled with curiosity as to past, present, and future events and ideas. This curiosity must be translated into testable concepts for which it is possible to design studies to support or refute those concepts. The distinction between a philosopher and a researcher is the latter's capability to garner evidence that is relevant to choosing between competing concepts or hypotheses.

To effectively execute research, it is essential that one has an open mind. A popular anecdote in research circles concerns the "intellectual who either found support for the claimed hypothesis or asserted that support would have been identified if only the measurement tools available were more precise." Such denial of contrary evidence is the epitome of unscholarly behavior and precludes learning.

One of the more difficult research "facts of life" is that while it is possible to disprove, it is impossible to prove. Inconsistent evidence clearly demonstrates a flaw in a concept; yet, consistent evidence can merely support the reasonableness of a concept—it cannot undeniably demonstrate that concept. The reason for the latter is that it is impossible to structure a study that controls for all possible influences upon a concept, and it could very well be the case that the very item omitted from the study would have altered the entire set of findings. An analogy to this fact of life is present in the typical auditing process when a statistical sample is drawn. In the absence of a 100 percent test, a point estimate cannot be provided at 100 percent confidence. Instead, we form confidence intervals, thereby acknowledging that a risk exists of the real number being outside our estimated range. However, just as most auditors are comfortable with a 95 percent confidence level, researchers are persuaded by statistically significant—as distinct from definitive—findings on research questions of interest.

This leads to a third set of extremely valued and interrelated traits for a researcher—patience, thoroughness, and perseverance. Very few findings are obvious in a research study over the short term. The scientific method demands a painstaking data collection and "clean-up process," familiarization with the data, and basic analysis of the data set as necessary steps toward the primary analysis of interest. Often, several "cuts of the data" must be performed before the factors of relevance to the research question can be isolated and quantified. The primary need for patience and thoroughness arises at the planning stage of the research, as the researcher must strive to identify all relevant factors and noise that are likely to pervade the data and that should be controlled to the extent possible and practical. The mode of measuring factors and controlling for noise must be tested for clarity in pilot samples or experiments if the likelihood of the success of the research is to be maximized. Perseverance is likely to be required in obtaining complete data sets for analysis. Often, the personal persistent contact with participants in the study is the most effective means of obtaining a complete quality data set.

The excitement of the research process, in large part, will depend on the researcher's ability to identify interesting research questions. Rarely does a study address only one issue, and the ability to identify by-products of the study and implications of the research for other researchers, as well as practitioners, is an important element of retaining the researcher's interest and attention to the project. For example, one might state that a study is directed at determining whether a correlation exists between the incidence of errors and the presence of certain management controls. However, that same study ought to be acknowledged as providing insights regarding:

- The types of errors commonly located in particular accounts and their magnitude, analyzed by industry.
- The effectiveness of various audit procedures in detecting such errors.
- The quality of documentation in the work papers regarding error detection.

This global, yet realistic, picture of the research project will attract and retain the interest of the researcher, the participants in the study, and supporters of the inquiry. No matter how long-range the research orientation, short-term by-products are likely to be available, enhancing our understanding of issues of current interest.

To place yourself in a research mode, list issues pertaining to the subject, such as auditing, about which you're curious. State those issues in the form of testable hypotheses or concepts. Then envision a way in which these issues might be tested. Consider the relevant factors requiring control and the probable problems that are expected to arise as you attempt to measure these factors.

Place yourself in a devil's advocate role and challenge the intended testing approaches. Why is this research unlikely to produce meaningful results? What is left out of the research design? How might the study produce ambiguous results? Is it impossible to measure or control for certain relevant factors or prevalent noise in the data? A cynic has suggested that when one is told there is no such thing as "can't," challenge that individual to eat an ice cream cone from the bottom to the top. In a sense, this same tenacity of listing the "can't's" is an essential step in the research process. The researcher should understand the flaws in any proposed study and strive to address as many of those flaws as is possible and practical.

As the "can't's" are itemized, the true researcher does not get depressed but, rather, recognizes the challenge of the investigation and the care that is necessary to perform meaningful research. While research must be structured, questions of interest are rarely structured, but must be made so by the researcher. While replications of prior research studies can be meaningful contributions, as can the use of readily available data sets, the most interesting research questions are likely to demand creative thought in providing structure and grueling efforts in data collection. Yet, as is usually the case, increased effort will bring increased reward in the sense that results will be interesting, the quality of the findings will be sound, and the contribution to knowledge will be substantial.

A common claim is that certain problems and issues are too complicated to be analyzed using experimental methods and statistical tools. Yet, a research-minded individual will define the complexity, consider how he or she thinks about the various dimensions of the problem or issue, and then match these thoughts with scales of measurement. While we may not be able to reach consensus that one control is expected to be 87 percent effective while another is 86 percent effective, it is likely that a 5- to 10-point classification scheme of control effectiveness could be designed with which relative rankings that mirrored judgments could be generated. Imagine the snail-paced evolution of science that would have resulted if scientists had laid aside the "complex" problems as unworkable. The social scientists should learn from the inductive research approaches of scientists. Scientists' observational skills in noticing how a fulcrum and lever operate, how bubbles form in beer, how a wagon moves up and down a hill, and how apples drop from trees all led to great strides in the sciences. Such skills need perfection in the social sciences (organizations involving people as distinct, for example, from the laws of physics), and surprising observations should be explored rather than dismissed as perverse results that must be due to some shortcoming in research design. If you believe there remain things to learn, you can be an effective researcher. Inductive research can be viewed as the process of putting a puzzle together, with only a general idea of what the final picture will be. The pieces of the puzzle will be empirical research, systematic observation, and the assimilation of related sets of evidence.

The final step in replicating the scientific method thought process is to structure some if/then analyses. If your evidence was _____, then your conclusion would be _____. The evidence that has been accumulated can then be evaluated as being either supportive or contrary to the original hypotheses. By thinking through such an if/then set of possibilities, problems in interpretation can be highlighted that may be resolvable by adjusting the research design.

It is probably fair to say that research strives to distinguish what we know from what we think we know and, in turn, from what we'd like to know. Often, experience is cited as the primary basis of professional judgments, and many companies and firms perform what is termed in-house research that relies heavily upon its professional staff's reported experiences. The relationship between anecdotal experience and formal research is that the latter strives to systematically analyze the former in a manner that controls for the types of bias that can inadvertently affect individuals' perceptions of the world. For example, if you asked 30 partners about how effective controls are at the average client, they would most likely insist that you give them a "context" and that you control for such important factors as the types of client that they typically audit—classified by industry code, size, and similar attributes. Trying to reach conclusions from observed behavior is extremely difficult and risky in the absence of a formal research design and plan for analysis. The systematic analysis of problems to increase our knowledge is the intent of research.

This analysis will involve the use of observation skills and research tools. In fact, the ability to identify and apply relevant research tools is an important dimension of being a researcher. However, a team approach is often the most practical means of acquiring such essential analytical and quantitative skills that, in turn, can be pooled with the observational and judgmental skills of others who are involved in the research endeavor in order to produce a meaningful research study.

How exactly can practitioners assist academic researchers in learning more about auditing practice and theory? One key mode of assistance is to inform researchers of unanswered questions that pose problems for practitioners. These problems may be short- or long-range and may entail such global questions as how materiality can be most effectively determined and allocated, or straightforward practice problems such as how multilocation sampling can be performed most efficiently yet provide a reasonable coverage of audit risk?

Beyond generating research questions, practitioners can be very helpful in providing critiques of proposed research studies. Is the question being addressed of consequence? Is the proposed research design capable of analyzing the problem, or have the issues been so oversimplified that any conclusions drawn would be suspect? Another effective means of evaluating a planned research approach is to participate in a pilot study and to help researchers identify holes in the analysis that are apparent to experienced auditors but might go unnoticed by the researcher. Practitioners have enormous databases that could be provided to researchers for analysis and expand our understanding of the audit process and the profession's social, economic, and legal environment. Beyond such direct involvement in research, the financial support of research is essential in providing the necessary resources for scientific inquiry. The joint effort of practitioners and researchers has a far better chance of increasing our level of knowledge than does unilateral effort by either party.[42]

CHAPTER 10

IMPLICATIONS

It is okay to forecast, as long as you don't do it in the future.

—*Mark Twain*[43]

In line with Mark Twain's sage advice, I will resist predicting future lines of inquiry, advanced research techniques that will inevitably evolve, or the undeniable role of technology in facilitating answers to previously unanswered questions. I will merely pause to comment that the information age, in large part facilitated by technology, is no doubt here to stay. As services of every variety increase in importance within the economy, information will be increasingly demanded to serve the needs of both the providers and recipients of such services. Global competition has increased awareness of the indispensable role of information to success.

Political battles are regularly fought in which the playing field is one of information streaming from various directions—often generated by vested interest groups. While knowing the source of information may make you wary of its credibility at times, far more than the source is relevant in evaluating the validity and persuasiveness of the evidence being presented. Economic battles in the marketplace and in the courtroom have similarly evolved into substantial amounts of information being prepared by adversarial parties, with an intent to persuade the consumer, jury, or judge. As one is bombarded by facts, figures, and representations, the question of whom I should believe is posed.

The concepts developed in this book provide a foundation for beginning to think critically about the information presented and how it was gathered, analyzed, and communicated. Streams of research have been briefly described to whet your appetite to pursue those ideas of particular interest. An appendix provides you with numerous definitions of terms, concepts, ideas, and evidence to date to help you comprehend various types of technical literature relating to those areas in which you wish to acquire specialized knowledge. You will likely find the described jargonese to be a useful reference for the long term.

The intent of this book is to sensitize you to potential sources of pollution in the information to which you are exposed. The idea is that being forewarned in some sense means forearmed to answer the question of primary interest: Do the facts speak for themselves?

APPENDIX

JARGONESE

An economist is a man who states the obvious in terms of the incomprehensible.

—*Alfred A. Knopf*[44]

This appendix provides a brief description of various terms that you may find referenced as you read research-related literature. If you fail to find a term of interest here, please refer to the key-word index, as ideas contained in the text are often not repeated herein.

a priori Before the facts are accumulated, a known or assumed cause is linked to an effect through theory; often used in discussing theory that is deductive or prescriptive in nature to permit clear hypotheses before any data are examined. (See ex ante.)

abnormal performance index (API) A predecessor to the cumulative abnormal returns concept. (See CAR.)

abnormal returns Or "excess returns" are returns over and above risk-adjusted return commensurate with an investment's beta (i.e., the firm's return after subtracting out those returns that are attributable to overall movements of the stock market). It is also possible to define abnormal returns as the difference in observed returns and the mean return for a sample period referred to as mean-adjusted returns—or as the difference in observed return and the market return.

adjusted R-square The explanatory power of a regression model, adjusted for the number of descriptive variables in a model, relative to the number of observations; it is possible for an adjusted R-square value to be negative, meaning that the model has no descriptive power; adjusted R-square is symbolized $\overline{R}^2$ and calculated as $1 - [(1 - R^2)(\frac{n-1}{n-k})]$ where n = number of observations, k = variables in a model plus the intercept, R^2 = R-squared; the adjustment is most important when n and k are close together.[45]

adverse selection A phenomenon that results whenever information is not produced and it is difficult or impossible for one party to otherwise assess the fulfillment of contractual terms or quality of some item being offered; since high quality cannot be distinguished from low quality by buyers (as an example), prices drop and only the worst quality is offered for sale; this is often referred to as the "market for lemons" and has been applied to the used car market[46] as exemplary of such a phenomenon.[47]

agent A party engaged as a steward to perform some service on others' behalf; commonly, performance requires the delegation of decision-making authority and the safeguarding of assets owned by others known as principals.

aggregation The adding together of items to present a more summarized form of information; such summations are more objectionable (in that they can lead to a substantial loss of information) when (1) the two items being combined form a large fraction of a related total (e.g., components of total assets on a financial statement) and (2) the two items are more equal to each other in magnitude.

alpha risk (α) See type I error.

alternative hypothesis That hypothesis that is to be accepted if the null hypothesis is rejected.

anchoring and adjustment A heuristic in which overreliance on prior knowledge (the anchor) leads to subsequent failure to sufficiently adjust judgments in light of new information.

ANCOVA (analysis of covariance) Modeling that includes a concomitant variable as a covariate in order to statistically control its effects; for example, a covariate might be the size of a firm when trying to study industry patterns.

ANOVA Analysis of variance; a multivariate (i.e., more than a single variable) analysis of main effects and interaction effects of a number of treatments (or variables) on an outcome; as an example, a survey of business managers' points of view as to causes of bankruptcy and warning signals can be analyzed to determine if certain opinions are affected by factors such as experience, gender, industry, and company size, or interaction among such variables—for example, for this industry, smaller companies' managers have different perceptions from larger companies' managers; ANOVA designs can eliminate multicollinearity and permit measurement of such interaction effects.

applied researcher A perspective that gives less priority to construct validity of the causal variable, statistical conclusions, and the construct validity of the affected variable; internal and external validity operationally receive highest priority.

archival research Concerned with recorded facts, for example, documents.

ARIMA (autoregressive integrated moving average) A term applied to a family of techniques that includes time-series tools such as Box-Jenkins and regression analysis; Figure 5 describes two common classes of time-series processes (see autocorrelation).

Arrow's impossibility theorem See impossibility.[48]

artificial intelligence A technology whose processes give computers the human-like abilities to see, hear, speak, and reason with imprecise or incomplete information, and learn.[49]

association That which can be demonstrated with statistics in other than an experimental setting; it simply ties movements of various measures together in either a positive (similar) pattern or in negative (inverse or opposite) directions.

associative memory Relates evidence to prototypes of problem solutions.

asymmetric Not balanced or harmonious proportions; for example, a stock issuer's inside information would represent asymmetric information in the marketplace relative to a purchaser's position.

autocorrelation A pattern among observations of a single data series; this concept underlies ARIMA and also is the term applied to a statistical problem in regression analysis which involves a pattern in residuals (the differences between estimated and actual observed values).

availability Decision makers' tendency to assess the probability by the ease with which instances are brought to mind.[50]

FIGURE 5
Time-Series Processes

Combine persistency characteristics of a constant-mean model with
the unpredictable behavior of a random-walk model

Autoregressive Processes
a tendency to revert to some mean level over long periods

Expected deviation of next
period's earnings from the
long-run average (if small,
constant-mean process is
observed)

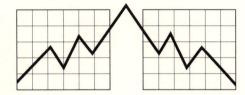

Smoothing Models (Moving Average Models are one subset)
partially eliminate or smooth out chance factors in reported numbers to provide a best
guess of earnings next period

Next period's earnings are
expected to be this period's
earnings adjusted by some
fraction of last period's
forecast error (as a smoothing
coefficient--if zero, random walk).

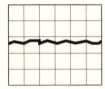

Adapted from Paul A. Griffin, *Research Report: Usefulness to Investors and Creditors of Information Provided by Financial Reporting.* 2nd ed. (Stamford, Conn.: Financial Accounting Standards Board, 1987), pp. 60–61.

axioms   Propositions that are accepted without a formal proof.

Bayesian models   A normative model that is appropriate for updating beliefs in light of new
evidence; prior information is combined with evidence to determine posterior probabilities
according to a specified Bayes's theorem; to exemplify:

$$(M|\bar{E}) = \frac{P(M)\,P(\bar{E}|M)}{P(\bar{E}|M)\,P(M) + P(\bar{E}|\bar{M})P(\bar{M})}$$

where

$$P(M) = \text{The prior probability of } M \text{ (prior odds or expected base rate)}$$
$$P(\bar{M}) = \text{The complement of } P(M), \text{ that is, } 1 - P(M)$$
$$\bar{E} = \text{Results of research evidence collected}$$
$$P(\bar{E}|M) = \text{Likelihood of } E \text{ given the state } M$$
$$P(M|\bar{E}) = \text{Posterior odds}$$

behavioral research A line of inquiry directed at understanding professional judgment with an intent of improving the effectiveness and efficiency of decision making.

beta Most commonly used as a risk measure; specifically, beta is measured as the relationship between an individual company's stock return and that of the market (often measured as the Standard & Poor's 500 stock return index or some similar market index): (*a*) a 1.0 beta would be a stock that effectively moved in tandem with the market, (*b*) a beta below 1.0 is characterized as lower systematic risk than the overall market, having fewer swings than the general market, and (*c*) beta in excess of 1.0 is characterized as higher systematic risk, having far more pronounced reactions than those of the general market (if expected excess return on a market portfolio is 10 percent, a security with a 2.0 beta would be expected to yield 20 percent; likewise, an expected market decline of 10 percent would be expected to result in a loss of 20 percent on that security).

beta risk (β) See type II error.

between-subjects design Focuses on differences of opinion of various individuals, one compared with another.

bias Systematic error, for example, "window-dressing" or a tendency to misstate (such as overstating earnings).

biases Distortion of judgments due to such effects as: retrievability of instances (i.e., a bias toward more retrievable analogies when making decisions); the effectiveness of a search set (or lack thereof); excessive imaginability; and illusory correlation (i.e., the appearance of two things being related because they happen to be affected by a common third factor).

Black-Scholes pricing model An equilibrium option pricing model that explains the determinants of an option's value prior to expiration, including the current price of the underlying stock, the exercise price, the volatility of stock returns, time to maturity, interest rates, and anticipated dividends.[51]

Blackwell's theorem States that more is better than less at zero cost.

blocking Removing or statistically controlling a concomitant variable by assuring an equal number of subjects is at each level of the blocking variable (the concomitant variable might be size, industry type, gender, or some similar attribute).

bonding costs Are incurred by the agent (the party responsible for others' resources) to guarantee that he or she will not take specified actions that would harm the principal or that the principal will be paid if the agent has taken such actions, for example, financial statement audits, explicit insurance, and limitations on power.

bootstrapping Assisting judgment with a "model of man," such as a regression model of basic decision rules; this term has also been applied to adjustments to statistical methods that are intended to address perceived shortcomings.

bounded rationality The theory of problem solving that contends individuals have limited knowledge and ability to analyze complex problems, hence they invoke heuristics to simplify the decision process;[52] extensions of this theory contend that short-term memory is assumed to be limited to four to seven "chunks," although long-term memory is assumed to be unlimited.

Box-Jenkins method A time-series analysis tool that evaluates data over time for a single variable such as sales, with the objective of identifying patterns and quantifying them for use in modeling and prediction.

brainstorming   Group sessions that focus on a single problem, consider any idea, avoid criticism of ideas, and do not explore the implication of any idea.[53]

Brunswik's lens model   A psychology-based model, with a right side representing predominant cues or information relied upon to make various decisions; studies tend to be descriptive, manipulating hypothesized cues to evaluate their effect on judgments;[54] the model can be depicted as follows:

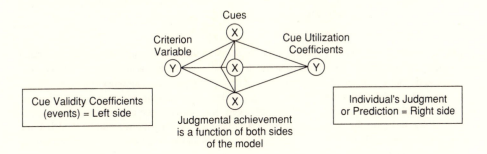

call option   A contract permitting owners to buy at their discretion a stated number of shares of an underlying security at a stated price (referred to as the exercise or striking price) on or before a set expiration date; such options are more valuable as the underlying security's price increases.

capital asset pricing model (CAPM)   A theoretical relationship of individual security prices to the overall market index, which expects returns to be risk-adjusted; commonly written as

$$E(R_i) = R_f + B_i [E (R_m) - R_f]$$

where

$$B_i = \frac{\text{cov} (r_i, r_m)}{\text{var} (R_m)}$$

R_i = Return on asset
R_f = Risk-free rate like the Treasury-bill rate
R_m = Market rate of return
cov = Covariance
var = Variance
E = Expectation

CAPM is derived under the assumptions that (1) a riskless security exists, (2) investors can borrow or lend unlimited amounts at this riskless rate, and (3) all investors have identical investment horizons and expectations about the distributions of the asset values at the end of this horizon (i.e., they agree on the expected value and the variability of returns, including covariances of returns among all securities). Other assumptions embodied in the model are that perfect capital markets exist in which investors are price takers, there are no taxes or transaction costs, all investors have equal and costless access to information, and the quantities of securities are fixed.

Cartesian product   The set of all ordered pairs that can be systematically constructed from their elements; underlies information analysis mathematical techniques.

causality   A claim that some attribute causes a particular effect that can only be made through experimental design; it is often inferred from other statistical analyses, but such an inference is distinct from what is actually demonstrable from a statistical perspective.

ceteris paribus   Everything else is assumed to be the same, that is, is held constant; this phrasing is intended to fulfill all causes that are not included in a given model.

characteristic line   See security market line.

Chi-square analyses   These are nonparametric statistics that do not require a normal distribution of a data set and can be applied to nominal (classification) data; as an example, a researcher could compare the incidence of changes in accounting principles among companies that did have financial difficulties relative to the incidence for companies without such financial difficulties, to see whether a pattern emerged, for example, are companies with financial difficulties more likely to have accounting changes? Such a pattern could be depicted in a contingency table with the cells marked expected to include a greater number of the sample observations (see contingency tables).

circularity   Reasoning X to Y and Y to X.

cluster analysis   A technique by which attributes of data points are compared and similarities and differences among such traits can be detected; clusters are identified by minimizing differences within groups and maximizing differences between clusters.

Cochrane Orcutt   An iterative regression modeling technique that is intended to address problems with autocorrelation in the residuals; in particular, the data set is differenced and weighted by a factor known as rho, which measures first-order autocorrelation.

coefficient of variation   The standard deviation divided by the mean, which measures the relative spread of a distribution around its mean.

coefficients   Quantities estimated in regression modeling and similar multivariate techniques that capture the change in the variable being explained by the model for every unit change in a particular descriptor or independent variable, holding everything else in the model constant; their sign indicates the direction of such relative movement, and the term *regression coefficients* is applied in regression models.

cognitive dissonance   The idea that decision makers become more comfortable with their judgments by rationalizing and defending them and lowering the status of the choices not selected.

cognitive use of the language   Communication of factual statements about the world.

collective choice rules   Satisfied by majority voting: (1) decisiveness, meaning that the preferred alternative between any pair is identifiable; (2) anonymity, meaning that the identity of individuals holding particular preferences is irrelevant; (3) neutrality, meaning the labeling of alternatives does not affect rules; and (4) positive responsiveness, meaning that ceteris paribus, if one individual changes preference toward an alternative, the rule likewise shifts favorably.

common interest theory   X is in the common interest means X is in the interest of all individuals; if not, nothing follows (that is the problem with the theory).[55]

compensatory model   The notion that one attribute in a judgment model can compensate for another; as an example, an investor may permit profitability to compensate for high risk and accept an investment, whereas others may not permit profitability to compensate for any risk level above "investment grade."

complete market   One in which a claim to receive $1 if one state occurs and receive nothing otherwise (i.e., primitive claims) can be traded; complex and compound claims' values can be inferred from their primitive claim components.[56]

completeness assumption   Used in modeling to guarantee that any information effects are strictly limited to probability revision, since all four facets of a decision model are assumed to be correctly specified. (See decision model.)

composite judge   The judgment of a group of individuals, rather than a single person; aggregation of only three judges can produce most of the accuracy advantage of such a basis for judgment.[57]

compounding   Interest is earned on interest as well as principal.

conjunctive model   Requires that some minimum level of performance be exceeded on all variables in the model and hence is a form of noncompensatory modeling.

consensus   The degree to which individual decision makers agree with one another.

conservatism   The tendency of subjects to revise their prior probabilities less than they should, according to Bayes's theorem.

contingency tables   These are commonly produced by CROSSTABS or similar routines in statistical packages and effectively compare classification variables to determine if the distribution of observations among cells in a matrix comparing two such variables is other than random; a four-celled table might compare companies having an accounting change to those not having an accounting change along the *y* axis, to companies experiencing financial difficulty to those not experiencing financial difficulty along the *x* axis; if the four cells of the resulting matrix are virtually the same in terms of the number of observations so classified, a random distribution is observed; however, if far more observations appear in the two diagonal cells, that is, those with financial difficulty have accounting changes, while those without accounting changes tend not to have financial difficulty, then an association has been identified; the significance of such a pattern can be measured through a Chi-squared statistic. (See Chi-squared statistic.)

continuous compounding Computed as the natural logarithm of the ratio of the investment's value at year-end to that at the beginning of the year.

contradictory results Likely to be due to a poorly conducted experiment or a lack of control of extraneous variables.

contrast or surprise effect Observed in the updating of decision makers' beliefs whereby the stronger an initial belief is held (the anchor), the more it is discounted by negative evidence (conflicting with the belief) and the less it is increased by positive evidence (confirming the belief).[58]

control group Used to describe a comparison group, thought to serve as a useful benchmark to evaluate the relationships of interest; for example, nonbankrupt companies could serve as a control group for evaluating the extent to which the incidence of a change in accounting practices in bankrupt companies is significantly greater.

convergent validity See elicitation theory.

corollaries A proposition that follows from a theorem, that is, because the theorem is known to be true, this proposition follows almost immediately.

corporate personality An intolerance for ambiguity or the need to avoid vague and undefined stimuli is thought to affect decisions such as how conservative the portfolio of accounting practices will be for a particular company.

correlation A statistical measure of how one variable moves in relation to another; the common parametric statistic (requiring the data distribution to be normal) is the Pearson product moment correlation and ranges from $+1$ to -1, where $+1$ is the correlation of every variable with itself, representing an identical pattern, and -1 is an opposite pattern where, as one variable increases, the other decreases, with 0 representing no correlation whatsoever; the Pearson correlation coefficient is the term sometimes used for this measure, which effectively assesses whether as one variable is observed to lie above its mean, is another variable observed to lie above or below its respective mean? Furthermore, how systematic is that pattern across a set of data points? The correlation coefficient is computed as the covariance standardized by division by the product of the two variables' standard deviation. (Note that nonparametric correlations that do not require an assumption of a normal distribution are available, including the Spearman and Kendall rank order correlation—these are computed from rankings in lieu of using mean values, since the latter's propriety depends on the underlying data set having a normal distribution.) See scatter diagrams.

counterbalancing A practice of varying the order of treatment among subjects to avoid an ordering effect; care must be taken not to confound the exposure of subjects to prior treatments with the number of measurements taken.

covariance A measure of the degree to which two variables move together, similar to the correlation variable, but its magnitude is difficult to interpret since it is influenced by the standard deviations of the variables being correlated; hence, other than its use in interpreting the direction of a relationship, this measure is typically standardized and reported as a correlation coefficient.

criterion variable See dependent variable.

cumulative abnormal return (CAR)   A summation of average abnormal returns over time, typically tied to some event that affects more than a single day of trading; the CAR is expected, on average, to be zero; this can be computed by using the market model, defined as $\tilde{R}_{it} = a_i + b_i \tilde{R}_{mt} + \tilde{\epsilon}_{it}$ as follows:

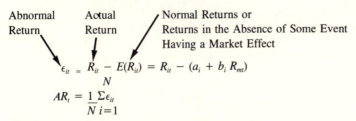

Abnormal Return   Actual Return   Normal Returns or Returns in the Absence of Some Event Having a Market Effect

$$\epsilon_{it} = R_{it} - E(R_{it}) = R_{it} - (a_i + b_i R_{mt})$$

$$AR_t = \frac{1}{N}\sum_{i=1}^{N}\epsilon_{it}$$

where

ϵ_{it} = Unsystematic (diversifiable) risk

R_{it} = Return on company i at time t

R_{mt} = Market return

a_i = Intercept obtained through regression modeling

b_i = A proxy for systematic (undiversifiable) risk—the tendency to move with the market index, commonly referred to as beta (see beta)

AR_t = Cross-sectional average abnormal returns

CAR = Cumulative abnormal return

Examples of patterns of CARs follow:

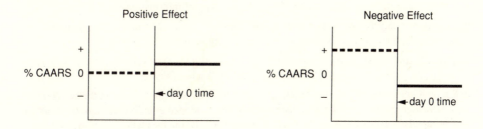

Positive Effect

Negative Effect

where

CAARS = Cumulative average abnormal returns

day 0 = Event of interest

decision model   A vehicle to characterize four common facets of decisions: (1) alternative resource commitments or decisions, referred to as acts (A); (2) possibilities of various states (S); (3) the probability function for the various states (Φ); and (4) preference encoding or utility specification (U). These facets combine with an existing level of experience (ξ) into a decision model, depicted as follows:

$(A,S,\Phi,U \mid \xi)$, which is said to be complete if all four facets are correctly specified.

deductive argument   Reasons from the general to the specific.

degrees of freedom The number of data points available to form a statistical estimate after recognizing the use of such data to generate specific statistical tests or parameters; in regression analysis, the number of observations less the number of parameters in the model (i.e., 1 for the intercept term, plus the number of independent or descriptor variables).

Delphi A method of obtaining experts' opinions, which entails: (1) elicitation of each expert's opinion; (2) collation of opinions and analysis to determine their consensus; (3) if no consensus, the other experts' opinions are communicated and the individuals' revised opinions are elicited; and (4) this process is repeated until consensus is reached or the process is terminated.

Dempster/Shafer belief function formalism A theory that assigns a probability measure to a related set (*a*) that bears on a set of relevant states (*b*), and then gathers evidence to assess the compatibility of the set of states and related set (i.e., (*a*) with (*b*)) with the degree of belief defined as the sum of probabilities of all elements of the related set that are compatible with only that state; this can be coupled with Bayes's Theorem and has been used in expert system development.[59]

dependent variable The variable of interest that is being explained by a regression model; also referred to as a Y-variable; the observation measured to obtain new information on the response to independent variables.

determinism The assumption of lawfulness in nature, enabling the identification of causes and patterns versus chaos.

disclosure index Compound index that sums the products of the perceived importance of a disclosure and the extent of disclosure.[60]

discovery information That which is a hidden property of nature so that only human action can extract it; accounting can be viewed as this type of information.

discriminant analysis A modeling technique intended to predict some classification that has two categories, such as bankruptcy versus no bankruptcy.

disjunctive models Require outstanding performance on at least one variable, but do not permit compensation of one variable for a minimum threshold of another.

dollar-unit sampling (DUS) A sampling method that automatically results in the selection of more high-dollar items, because the sampling unit is defined as individual dollars within an accumulated total of dollar balances of a relevant population; the method eliminates the need for dollar-based stratification, is effective in low error-rate and skewed populations, and is nonparametric in nature—when in its simplest form, requiring no distributional assumptions about the population (beyond the dollars obeying a binominal, hypergeometric, or multinomial process).[61]

drifts in stock prices Term applied to delayed adjustment of stock prices; cited as potentially raising a question of market inefficiency, although also attributed to differential firm characteristics.

dummy variables A term used to refer to a variable that typically assumes values of zero or one to represent some qualitative attribute(s) or nominal scale. For example, consider the codings: is a bankrupt company (1) or is not a bankrupt company (0); is a reorganized company (1) or is not a reorganized company (0). These two variables in a single model would control for three factors—bankrupt, reorganized, or other type of company; the

regression coefficients for these two dummy variables estimate systematic differences between the classifications for which dummy variables are included in the regression model
(i.e., bankrupt or reorganized companies) and that classification for which the dummy
variable is omitted (i.e., neither bankrupt nor reorganized). Note that one less than the
number of classifications is the maximum number of variables for which a regression model
can form regression estimates.[62]

economic consequences   A term applied to the cost-benefit effects of some event, such as the
reactions of the market to a change in an accounting principle.

efficient-market hypothesis   The concept that security market prices instantaneously reflect all
publicly available information is referred to as the semistrong form of market efficiency,
while the weak form relates only to historical price information, and the strong form to all
information.[63]

elicitation theory   A line of inquiry as to how to obtain individuals' subjective probability
assessments; the degree to which various techniques produce similar results is referred to
as convergent validity.

empirical research   Something that is based on observation or experience.

entropy   Expected information content of forthcoming messages; increases as probabilities
become more equal and the number of possible outcomes increases.

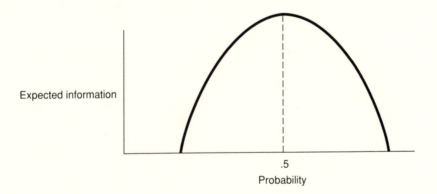

environmental criterion   What is the correct judgment?[64]

error of the third kind   Misapplication of statistical procedures.[65]

event studies   Statistical techniques for analyzing the pattern of stock prices and returns when
a special event occurs; these studies examine stock returns for some specific firms (or for
an industry) before and after the announcement of a special event, such as a merger;[66] key
steps in such studies include identifying the event and the date on which it occurred, estimat-
ing abnormal returns, grouping of abnormal returns, and then analyzing the data.

ex ante   A forecasting orientation; before the fact (it therefore often precludes specified factors).

ex post   After the fact; this type of analysis allows more causal-type factors to be considered
since hindsight is available.

existential hypothesis   Asserts that the relationship stated in the hypothesis holds for at least one particular case.

experimental markets   A research approach that uses an experimental setting of a market process, such as a double auction bid on information to infer its value.

expert system   Uses a knowledge base that has been coded from human experts' thinking process (one subfield of artifical intelligence); such systems try to capture the reasoning and decision-making processes of human experts with computer programs, often reasoning heuristically (with experts' rules of thumb) and justifying their conclusions after contemplating multiple competing hypotheses simultaneously.[67]

external validity   The extent to which the results of any one study can be generalized; the persistence of results as specific details of a single study are varied (e.g., who the subjects are in the study).

externality   Exists when one party's actions affect others who are not compensated (or charged) through some sort of pricing vehicle; this is a form of market failure.[68]

F-test   This is a statistical test most frequently used to compare variances (dispersion measures) of two samples; the F-test is typically used to measure whether the proportion of variance explained by a regression model is statistically significant.

factorial design   A simple design involves the conduct of two two-group experiments simultaneously, using two independent variables; the possible combinations of main effects and interactions in a 2x2 factorial design with two independent variables can be depicted as follows:

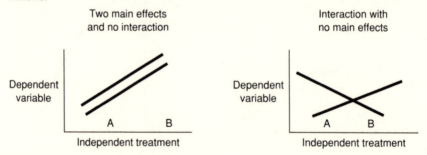

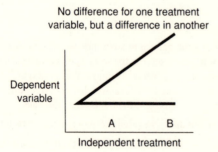

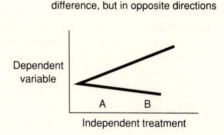

(An example this could reflect would be whether a treatment of (A) a change in accounting for inventory and (B) a change in bond rating affected the probability of bankruptcy (i.e., the dependent variable).) A completely crossed factorial design includes all unique combinations of cue values (i.e., of independent variables).

fault trees An engineering tool that analyzes the possible things that can go wrong and what could have caused such a problem to facilitate an evaluation by a problem solver.

fineness Information content in the absence of unintentional errors.

first differencing The practice of subtracting adjacent observations to convert the raw data in levels form to a first-differenced form, often to create a stationary series or to remove autocorrelation problems in regression modeling.

foreknowledge Information that is expected in advance and determined without further effort, such as weather information that is revealed by nature itself.

framing of decisions The judgment context encountered by a decision maker; the way in which questions are framed (data are presented, etc.) as to acts, contingencies, and outcomes influences the perception of what the nature of the problem is and related decisions.[69]

free riders Nonpaying users that result in underproduction of a good; the problem is that those who have not paid for a commodity cannot be excluded from its use (this commodity most likely has public-good attributes).

functional fixation People's tendency to stick to previously used ways of evaluating information, because they fail to recognize changes in context (or applicable algorithms) that should influence their decisions.

fuzzy set theory A methodology of probability intended to deal with vague concepts such as *fairness*.[70]

gambler's fallacy Self-correcting hypothesis.[71]

game theory A process of modeling decisions, given an individual is faced by a thinking opponent.[72]

grounded theory The idea of inductively developing theory, based on empirical observations; descriptive and predictive theory is discovered from data, often in natural settings.[73]

halo effects Positive bias caused by favorable past experiences; for example, a sound borrower in the past might be scrutinized less carefully than would be an applicant for a loan with whom there had been no past positive experience.

heteroscedasticity A statistical problem that means that the error in estimation across observations is not homogeneous; this can be caused by an omitted variable such as the inability to control for seasonality or size of operations.

heuristics Rules of thumb that simplify decision making but that may create distortions, such as giving too much importance to immediately-available information (see availability); yet, a heuristic solution can approximate an optimal solution.

hierarchical analysis One in which the inclusion of a higher-order interaction term implies that all lower-order terms are included; this would suggest that all main effects that comprise interaction terms are analyzed.

hindsight bias Created by a knowledge of outcomes that inhibits one's ability to recall accurately from memory or to imagine one's decision making without such knowledge.

homoscedasticity A desired characteristic of residuals in a regression model that means they have similar scatter (standard error or dispersion around zero).

illusory correlations The appearance of two things being related because they happen to be affected by a common third factor.

imperfect markets Those in which market prices may not fully reflect individuals' preferences.

impossibility theorem Arrow's demonstration that a group utility function that meets all criteria needed to be pareto optimal cannot be defined—specifically, the group utility assessment cannot meet the mutually inconsistent requirements of universal domain, pareto optimality, independence of irrelevant alternatives (i.e., ignore unavailable alternatives, ignore the intensity of preference, and rule out interpersonal utility comparisons), and nondictatorship.

incomplete markets Those in which some primitive claims cannot be traded and their value cannot be inferred from more complex claims (see complete markets).

independent variable A variable that is used to describe another variable of primary interest; it controls for aspects of the environment and measures how such aspects relate to reactions or changes in the dependent variable; often the independent variable is described as an x-variable and as treatments (in which case they may be manipulated rather than merely measured in natural settings).

indifference curve A representation of combinations of risk and return that are equally valued; if return is on the vertical axis, a convex shape would represent risk aversion.

individual decision-making framework Disaggregation into eight key elements: (1) task definition, (2) internal information acquisition (from memory), (3) external information acquisition (from other sources), (4) information processing, (5) output, (6) action, (7) outcome, and (8) feedback (i.e., the observed or communicated reaction to phases of the decision process).[74]

induction Fact finding or observation that leads to the generation of theory; such an approach tends to seek answers to questions of who, what, where, when, which, how, whether, and why.[75]

information content Increases as probability gets smaller and surprise (unexpectedness) gets larger.

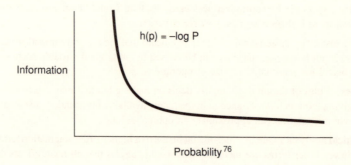

$$h(p) = -\log P$$

Information

Probability [76]

information-evaluation process Involves the decision maker's utility, the information system at hand and perceptions as to how signals from such a system are generated, the perception of the decision maker's prediction and choice process, and the perception of future states; these components interact in the evaluation process.[77]

information system   An information system is said to be useful if an act changes due to its application; the utility measure (U) of an information system (n) can be symbolized as:
$$E(U|n) = \Sigma\Phi\ (y|n)E(U|y,n)$$
where Φ = the probability function for the various states, $y = n(s)$, E = expected value, and s = state; the choice of information system should consider cost ($C(n)$) and will likely depend on alternatives, tastes, and beliefs.

institutional prices   Terms of trade attached to factors of production.

interactions   Joint effects of independent variables; the direction and magnitude of the relationship of two variables depend on the value of one or more other variables; also referred to as having a moderating effect.

internal validity   The extent to which variation in the dependent variable (i.e., the observed effect) can be really attributed to variations in the independent variable(s) (treatments); causality attribution.

interval scale   Consists of equal-sized units so that the distance between any two positions is of a known size.

intervening variable   A predictor of a dependent variable that is simultaneously predicted by an independent variable(s).

January effect   The name applied to the phenomenon that stock returns in January have been significantly higher than in other months (note, however, that these are raw returns).

Kendall coefficient of concordance (W)   A nonparametric test often used to determine the level of agreement among judges.[78]

knowledge   Currently held warrantable beliefs of concerned, reasonable, and creatively skeptical persons.[79]

Kohlberg's stages of ethical cognition   Stage 1, preconventional: avoid breaking rules backed by punishment in order to avoid such punishment; Stage 2, preconventional: follow rules when they are in one's own interest in order to serve one's own immediate interest; Stage 3, conventional: living up to what is expected by people in order to fill a need to be a good person; Stage 4, conventional: fulfilling agreed-to duties and obligations in order to keep the institution going; Stage 5, postconventional: uphold nonrelative obligations first in order to fulfill an obligation to law before social contracts; Stage 6, postconventional: follow self-chosen ethical principles in order to fulfill a belief in the ideal as a rational person.[80] This is a theory that has served as a basis for studying a variety of questions concerning ethics, including those suggested in Figure 6; yet, a point to ponder is whether we can ethically perform ethics-related research.

lemma   A preliminary proposition that is to be used in a proof of a theorem (each supporting lemma is a piece of a proof of a theorem).

lens model   See Brunswik.

logit analysis   A modeling technique that produces the probability of some event, such as the likelihood of bankruptcy.

main effects   Independent effects of independent variables.

FIGURE 6
Ethics-Related Research Questions

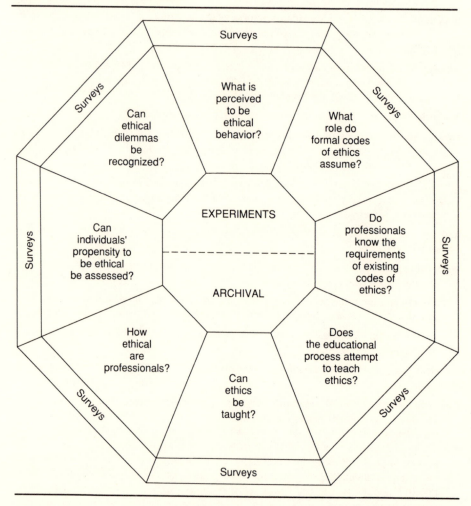

Mann-Whitney   A test that computes the difference between two samples by focusing on rank as a means of avoiding reliance on parametric statistics that use mean values and assume a normal distribution; this nonparametric test assumes ordinal measurement and is used to test whether two independent groups have been drawn from the same population.[81]

MANOVA (multivariate analysis of variance)   Multivariate statistical procedure that considers all dependent variables simultaneously (whereas ANOVA has a single dependent variable).

market model   An empirical tool used to apply the capital asset pricing model, which is described as:

$$\tilde{R}_{it} = a_i + b_i \tilde{R}_{mt} + \tilde{\epsilon}_{it}$$

where

$\tilde{R}_{it}$ = Rate of return to company i at time t

a_i = Intercept (regression parameter)

b_i = A proxy for systematic (undiversifiable) risk, determined as a regression parameter

$\tilde{R}_{mt}$ = Market index at the time t such as Standard and Poor's 500 stock index for the market return

$\tilde{\epsilon}_{it}$ = Unsystematic (diversifiable) risk error term for time period t

matching   A research technique that assures some variable's distribution is similar across levels of the independent variables; in a study comparing bankrupt companies to nonbankrupt companies, it is common to match along the dimensions of size and industry classification.

mathematical symbols   Commonly used in proofs

Symbol	Meaning
$=>$	implies
$<=>$ (iff)	if and only if
ϵ	is an element of
$\underline{c}$	subset
ϕ	empty set
$\sim$	not
$\forall$	for all (for each, etc.)
$\exists$	there is (there are, etc.)
$\ni$	such that
$\wedge$	and
$\vee$	or
Q.E.D.	quod erat demonstrandum (which was to be demonstrated)[82]

mean   Average value that is computed by taking the sum and dividing by the number of observations.

metaphysical problem   Unsolvable since testable propositions are not possible; hence, these are not empirically demonstrable.

minimalist theories   If any X is not more in the interest of some individual theory, it is not more in the public interest.

model   Some representation of reality that is simpler than what is being emulated but is expected to have some explanatory power; models may be descriptive or theoretically derived.

monitoring costs   Include outside audits, budget constraints, and control systems; these are intended to assure the principal that the agents take actions desired by the principal.

moral hazard   Shirking activities by agents or other actions taken by agents other than those that would have been specified by the principal if such specification were possible.

moral reasoning   Differs from other judgment in that (1) cognition is grounded in value rather than tangible fact, (2) judgment is based upon some issue involving self and others, and (3) judgment is framed around an issue of "ought" rather than being based upon simple likings or preference rankings.

multiattribute problems Those involving a number of well-identified aspects or alternatives, such as market standing, innovation level, productivity, physical and financial resources, profitability, manager development, and public responsibility in business settings.[83]

multicollinearity A statistical concern in modeling (particularly regression analysis), which refers to the possibility that descriptor variables are intercorrelated among themselves in an unstable manner, leading to difficulty in the interpretation of specific coefficients in a model.

multidimensional scaling A geometric distance model that is useful in exploratory research or when cues are ill-defined; it expresses relationships between objects.

multiple comparisons test Statistical tool used to compare several averages, one to the other, to identify which differences are statistically significant.

multivariate normality A distribution involving at least three variables in which the distribution of one variable is normal for each and every combination of categories of all other variables.

multivariate techniques Statistical tools that consider more than a single variable; for example, multiple regression analysis with two or more independent variables is a multivariate technique (bivariate means two variables at a time).

nested or hierarchical variables Those that are not crossed or represented in all levels of other between-subjects variables; preferably, different subjects in each group represent subjects nested in treatment groups; if differences among groups are observed, then the group must be the subject for analysis.

Newcomb's problem A conflict demonstrable in game theory that presents a conflict between dominance reasoning and expected-utility reasoning (if sufficient probabilistic dependence between agents' choices is induced in the prisoner's dilemma, this paradox emerges).[84]

news-conditional residual returns The result of applying a modeling approach that controls for the number of news announcements, along with the more typical parameters of the capital asset pricing model.[85]

nexus of contracts An approach to viewing firms that has been criticized as insufficient in not allowing differentiation between consumers, firms, or markets, or explaining why an intermediary is created for contracting; this may lead to future attention to relative contracting costs.

noise Unintentional error.

noiseless A characteristic of information systems, which means that one and only one signal or message is associated with each state.

nominal measurement A classification or category variable, rather than a rank or continuous variable; no quantitative relationships or ordering among classes is implied.

noncompensatory models Those that do not permit a shortcoming along one attribute to compensate for another; a bank might require both liquidity and quality accounts receivable, as measured by the average receivable turnover ratio before a loan is granted, i.e., great liquidity but poor turnover is unacceptable.

nonlinearity   Other than a linear relationship; in regression modeling, nonlinearity can be estimated using natural logarithms, square roots, and exponents, such as squared relationships; reciprocals can be used to capture asymptotic relationships, that is, those with a ceiling or floor.

nonorthogonal designs   Those in which independent variables become dependent and correlated.

nonparametric statistics   Refer to a body of statistics not requiring the normal distribution assumption or similar constraints applicable to parametric statistics, such as the *t*-test.[86]

normal distribution   A smooth, symmetrical shape of a data set that is totally defined by its average value (see mean) and its standard deviation (dispersion around the mean).

normative research   Intended to be prescriptive in identifying what should be done (in accounting, examples of normative criteria are relevance to decision makers and reliability of measurement).[87]

null hypothesis   The hypothesis of no differences that is formulated for the express purpose of rejecting it.[88]

ordinal scale   A set of ordered classes into which cases can be sorted so that each has a greater than, equal to, or less than relationship to every other case.

orthogonal designs   Those in which the independent variables are totally independent or uncorrelated.

outlier   A case that deviates substantially from some measurement of central tendency, such as the mean, or from the regression estimate formulated.

overfitting   The possibility of tailoring a descriptive model so closely to the data set from which it is formulated that it becomes less useful in explaining interrelationships of other data.

p-**value**   A term applied to the probability or significance level determined by a statistical test; how improbable an event could be under the null hypothesis.

pareto efficient   A result that makes at least one person better off without making anyone worse off.

perfect markets   A concept meaning that (1) the trading of commodities and claims take place at zero transactions costs, (2) no advantage exists to a firm or individual that would lead to the earning of abnormal returns, and (3) prices are invariant to any one individual's or firm's actions.[89]

policy makers' uses of research   (1) shaping perceptions; (2) examining assertions; (3) assessing consequences; (4) recording results; (5) determining acceptability; (6) identifying alternatives.[90]

positive economics   An approach independent of ethical positions or normative judgment, focusing on what *is* rather than what *ought to be* and generalizing to produce predictions to conduct objective science and achieve simplicity and fruitfulness; it matters little how realistic assumptions are, but it matters how sufficient an approximation these are for the purpose at hand.

postannouncement drifts   Tendency for stock market returns to drift slowly back to their original level after a key event.

power efficiency   Increase in sample size that would be necessary to make a test as powerful as a specified other test.

power of tests 1-beta (type II error).

pragmatic use of the language Intended to produce changes in the world by affecting the action or behavior of people in preconceived ways: commands, prescriptions, and recommendations. These have an ethical dimension.

precision Accuracy; the degree of refinement in objective measurement.

prejudice against the null Greater propensity for submission to journals when null is rejected and to continue research when "close" to rejection of the null.

preponderance theory If X more than Y is in the interest of a preponderance of the society, then X is more in the public interest than Y, for example, majority rule.

price protection The principals' ability to protect themselves against agents' actions that are not in the principals' best interests, through pricing mechanisms, such as the agent's salaries. This explains why agents are willing to incur monitoring and bonding costs as a vehicle to increase their salaries, as this strategy can be expected to decrease principals' tendency to price-protect themselves.

principal A party who delegates others to perform some service on their behalf; often the holder of resources who contracts with an agent, directed to safeguard and enlarge the pool of assets with which the agent is entrusted.

probability density function A graph that depicts the shape of probabilities attached to some event, with an area under the curve equivalent to 1 (or 100 percent); as an example, consider the hypothetical distribution of the probability of occurrences of accounting changes [PCC]:

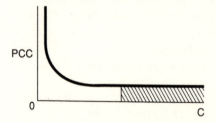

PCC

0

C

represents the probability of occurrence in any one year of the number of accounting changes exceeding five (approximately three percent)

probit analysis A modeling technique that predicts ordinal categories, such as bond ratings.

process-tracing tools Pegboards, video tapes, computers, and eye movement are among the tools used to trace the judgment process as a vehicle for obtaining knowledge from which expert system tools or other decision aids can be constructed; such tools are used to monitor auditors' information search behavior (acquisition of information, duration of search, and overall strategy).

proof A method of communicating a mathematical truth; a proof properly presented will contain no ambiguity.[91]

proposition A true statement of interest that you are trying to prove.

prospect theory Decision makers acquire information and encode it relative to some natural reference point (such as gains or losses relative to one's current wealth position) leading to differences in later evaluation of such information, depending on how a problem is framed;

a *positive framing* refers to a gain and will induce risk-averse behavior, whereas a negative framing, which refers to a loss, will induce risk-seeking behavior.[92] As depicted, the S-shaped, concave above the reference point and convex below it imply that a gain from $10 to $20 is greater than one from $110 to $120 and that any displeasure at losing is greater than the pleasure at winning.[93]

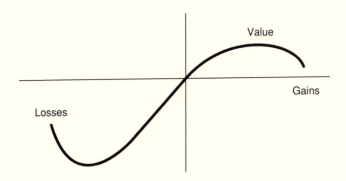

protocol analysis Process-tracing research in which subjects are asked to "think aloud"; then their accounts are analyzed in order to examine all phases of the process, from start to finish. This technique has been used to develop expert systems—criticisms include its subjectivity, the tendency for small sample sizes to be used, and high costs related to voluminous data collection and analysis.

public good Exists whenever one person's consumption of a good does not reduce another person's consumption; national defense is often cited as an example of such a good since use by one party does not diminish use by another party.

put option A contract entitling owners to sell a number of shares in an underlying security at their discretion, at a specified price, on or before a set expiration date; these shares increase in value as the underlying security's price decreases.

Q.E.D. See mathematical symbols.

quasi-experimental design Use of an ex post facto design that takes data as it is in the environment, without directly manipulating variables as would be common in an experimental design.[94]

R-square Percentage of variation in the variable of interest (dependent variable) that is explained by a model; the statistic must lie between zero and one, representing no explanatory power or perfect explanatory power, respectively, by a regression model—as an example, a regression model intended to explain sales as a function of number of customers and the consumer price index might explain 40 percent of the variation in sales across time (i.e., the time period used for estimation).

random selection Each element in the relevant population has a known and positive probability of selection.

random walk The current price of a commodity is also an unbiased estimate of its future price; no discernible pattern emerges, and successive changes are statistically independent. The random walk hypothesis means that, at a given point in time, the size and direction of the next price change is random since all available knowledge has been reflected at that point in time because changes in prices are random.

randomization Assignment to experimental and control groups in a manner not intended to cause any patterns, that is, ensuring against bias by distributing a variable across levels of the independent variables.

rational expectations An economic concept that assumes people take into account all available information that influences the outcome of their decisions, that they utilize this information intelligently, and, therefore, that they do not systematically make mistakes; people will learn from past mistakes and experiences and on average cannot be consistently fooled.

regression artifacts See regression toward the mean.

regression toward the mean The tendency for an observation to be less extreme than the data points generating that value, assuming the underlying process is stable.

reliability The ability to achieve the same result in replications of a research project.

representation hypothesis People believe samples to be very similar to one another and the population.

representativeness Probabilities are evaluated by the degree to which A is representative of B (i.e., one resembles another)[95]; a sort of stereotypical judgment.

residual The difference between a regression estimate and the actual value of that which is being estimated.

residual loss The reduction in the principal's welfare, which is the cost of the agency relationship, regardless of agency costs incurred.

risk aversion A strictly concave utility function that displays decreasing marginal utility; incentives are necessary to induce such a party to gamble.

risk neutrality A positive linear utility function, where decision makers are indifferent to risk.

runs test A test that discerns other than a random pattern in a sequence of data; for example, in regression analysis, a runs test is applied to the sign of the regression residuals to discern autocorrelation.

sample-size biases A tendency to disregard the effect of sample size on the variance of the sampling distribution; this tendency has been attributed to the heuristic of representativeness.

satisficing Behavior that stems from bounded rationality: in lieu of optimizing, merely requiring an acceptable decision.

scale validation Four concepts are used to validate scales: (1) face validity, (2) content validity, (3) predictive validity, and (4) construct validity.

scatter diagrams Pictures of data sets that are often used to discern correlations, as illustrated in Figure 7.

security market line The market return at a beta equal to 1, derived with the capital asset pricing model and illustrated as follows:

FIGURE 7
Examples of Scatter Diagrams

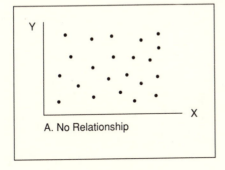

A. No Relationship

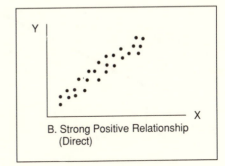

B. Strong Positive Relationship
(Direct)

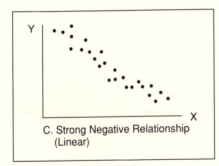

C. Strong Negative Relationship
(Linear)

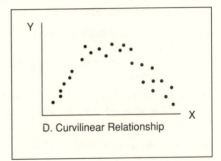

D. Curvilinear Relationship

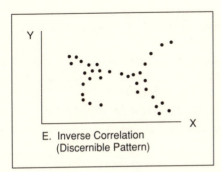

E. Inverse Correlation
(Discernible Pattern)

Source: Wanda A. Wallace, *Auditing* (New York: Macmillan, 1986), p. 419.

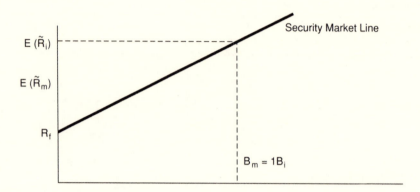

serial correlation Measures the association between two elements in a time series separated by a constant number of periods. (See autocorrelation.)

signalling A kind of implicit guarantee; a seller or other party giving a signal engages in some supplemental activity that would be irrational were his or her claims inaccurate; dividend practices of companies, as well as disclosure practices, have been interpreted to be forms of signalling.

significance level The probability that this result could happen by chance; a widely used significance level is .05, with the idea that a .05 value or less suggests statistical significance at a conventionally accepted level.

skewness An asymmetrical distribution.

small-firm effect The name applied to the empirical finding that small firms tend to have higher abnormal returns than do larger firms.

smoothing A term applied to an income-smoothing theory that management's choice of accounting procedures and their application are attempts to mitigate fluctuations about a normal level of earnings.

source credibility The effect of data reliability on judgment, based on how it is obtained; for example, a forecast of bankruptcy by an experienced financial analyst would be expected to be given greater weight than a forecast by an inexperienced evaluator.

spectral analysis A statistical method of testing for cyclical behavior in time series.

standard deviation The sum of squared deviations from the mean, which is intended to describe the dispersion in a data set.

standard error The sampling concept related to standard deviation for a population; this quantity gives credit for the sample size used to generate an estimate of the sample mean and then describes the dispersion estimated for such a mean by considering multiple selections from the population; in regression analysis, this concept is effectively the sum of squared deviations from the regression line, again appropriately adjusted to reflect the sample size.

state-probability specification Likelihood encoding.

state(s) Uncontrollable determinants of outcome (for example, the quality control over a particular product).

structured audit methodology A systematic approach to auditing that is characterized by a prescribed, logical sequence of procedures, decisions, and documentation signs, and by a comprehensive and integrated set of audit policies and tools; measured in one study by examining 18 elements related to planning, programs, controls, tools, documentation and review, and the overall audit process.[96]

synergy The sum of the parts is greater than the whole (often characterized as $2 + 2 = 5$); the notion that joint inputs come together in team production.

systematic risk An undiversifiable component of total risk, measured by beta, which relates individual security returns to the overall market return.

_t_-test A statistical test used to evaluate the difference between the average values of two samples; a paired sample _t_-test compares two averages taken on the same sample at different points in time.

taxonomy Classification system, such as types of research methods.

theorem A proposition, or true statement of interest that you are trying to prove, that you have subjectively considered to be extremely important (e.g., due to its predictive power).

threats to external validity These include representativeness of a sample after pretests, self-selection bias, experimental effects, irrelevance of independent variables, and motivation of subjects.[97]

threats to internal validity These include history, maturation, instability, testing, instrumentation, regression artifacts, selection, and experimental mortality.[98]

transformations Changes to values of a variable by applying some mathematical operation such as taking natural logarithms or square roots.

trialability of change Divisibility or the extent to which an innovation can be implemented on a partial basis; a characteristic that is advantageous to gaining the adoption of change, such as reaction to proposed accounting standards.

trimming the sample Deleting the most deviant observations.

truth table A method for determining when a complex statement is true by examining all possible truth values of the individual statements. For example, if someone asserted "If an accounting principle is changed, then bankruptcy will occur in two years," consider in what cases A implies B where A is the change in principle and B is bankruptcy. If both apply, then the truth has been told. However, if A occurs and B does not, then the truth has not been told. In the absence of a change in accounting principle, you could not establish that the assertion was not true. Hence, the associated truth table is as follows:[99]

A	B	A implies B
True	True	True
True	False	False
False	True	True
False	False	True

type I error If a hypothesis claimed that financial statements are fairly stated, and evidence suggested they were not, even though the true state of nature was that the statements were fairly presented, the auditing literature would view this as a type I error; it is viewed as an efficiency problem since it is assumed that if more extensive auditing were applied, the true state of nature would be apparent; by statistical convention, a type I error arises when a true null hypothesis (the assertion being tested) is incorrectly rejected and the probability of such an error is alpha risk.

type II error If a hypothesis claimed that financial statements are fairly stated, and evidence suggested they were, yet the true state of nature was that they were materially misstated, then the auditing literature would view this as a type II error; it is viewed as an audit effectiveness problem; by statistical convention, a type II error arises when a false null hypothesis is incorrectly accepted and the probability of such an error is beta risk.

type III error Failure to study the right issue.[100]

type IV error Lack of timeliness.[101]

unitary theories of public interest A unitary scheme of moral judgments guides individuals, making it impossible for individual interest to conflict with public interest.

universal domain condition Pareto optimality, whereby a complete and transitive ranking of available alternatives is prepared in order to provide a group utility measure.

unsystematic risk Diversifiable component of risk, representing company-specific risk exposure beyond the relationship of company return to market return.

utilitarianism A theory that evaluates social welfare by adding the utilities of individuals.[102]

utility specification [U(s,a)] A numerical encoding of preferences; preference precedes utility, with a utility function being unique, up to a positive linear transformation; note that such rankings are not useful for interpersonal comparisons.

Vs and Zs Other factors preceding or concurrent with the relationship of primary interest that, very likely, have not been controlled.[103]

validity Correspondence to reality or representativeness of that which is claimed to be represented.

variance Sampling variability in small numbers is underplayed.[104]

verbal protocols Means of collecting information on decision behavior by asking subjects to "think aloud" as they perform some task.

voter's paradox The idea that the order of voting, if known, can permit manipulation of the outcome; for example, if an agenda is to vote between x and y and then to compare the winner to z and a voter prefers x to y to z but knows x has no chance, that voter can ensure that y wins over z by voting against x.

weightings observed that differ from expected value (1) Impossible events are discarded; (2) low probabilities are overweighted; moderate and high probabilities are underweighted, with the latter more pronounced than the former; (3) probabilities that are low have a ratio of decision weights closer to unity.[105]

Wilcoxon test A statistical test to identify differences between two populations that have been paired in some manner; note that this is a nonparametric test that does not require a normal distribution.

Winsorizing the sample   Resetting extremes to less extreme values.

within-subjects design   Focus on changes in one's opinion before versus after some treatment.

Y-bar ($\bar{Y}$)   A term for the average value of the dependent variable in a regression model; note that *bar* is a notation for average and is merely a straight line above the letter.

Y-hat ($\hat{Y}$)   A term used to refer to the estimate formulated from a regression model.

weekend effect   Nomenclature used to refer to the empirical finding that Fridays are a good day to buy and Mondays a good day to sell.[106]

NOTES

1. James Charlton, ed., *The Executive's Quotation Book—A Corporate Companion*, (New York: St. Martin's Press, 1983), p. 18.
2. *Keely v. Westinghouse Electric Corp.*, 404 F. Supp. 573 (E.D. Mo. 1975), cited by David Whitten, "Statistics and Title VII Proof: Prima Facie Case and Rebuttal," *Houston Law Review*, May 1978, pp. 1030–53.
3. Darrell Huff (pictures by Irving Geis), *How To Lie with Statistics* (Norton: New York, 1954), 142 pages.
4. Cited by William D. Hall, *Accounting and Auditing: Thoughts on Forty Years in Practice and Education* (Chicago: Arthur Andersen, 1987), p. 31.
5. M. Friedman, "The Methodology of Positive Economics," *Essays in Positive Economics* (Chicago: University of Chicago Press, 1953); and D. D. McClelland, "Causal Explanation and Model Building in Economics," *Causal Explanation and Model Building in History/Economics and the New Economic History* (Ithaca, N.Y.: Cornell University Press, 1975).
6. Will Rogers quoted in Adam Smith, *Paper Money* (New York: Summit Books, 1981).
7. The popular book *A Brief History of Time: From the Big Bang to Black Holes* by Stephen W. Hawking (Toronto: Bantam Books, 1988) provides numerous examples of such evolution in physics, astronomy, and the natural sciences.
8. Richmond Campbell, "Background for the Uninitiated," in *Paradoxes of Rationality and Cooperation: Prisoner's Dilemma and Newcomb's Problem*, ed. Richmond Campbell and Lanning Sowden (Vancouver, B.C.: The University of British Columbia Press, 1985), pp. 1–4. For a discussion of means of addressing such a paradox, see Fred M. Frohock, *Rational Association (Syracuse, N.Y.: Syracuse University Press, 1987)*.
9. F. J. McGuigan, *Experimental Psychology: Methods of Research*, 4th ed. (Englewood Cliffs, N.J.: Prentice-Hall, 1983), p. 23.
10. David B. Smith and Susan Pourciau, "A Comparison of the Financial Characteristics of December and Non-December Year-End Companies," *Journal of Accounting and Economics*, 1988, pp. 335–44.
11. Altman's model combines ratios using accounting and market data reflecting liquidity, profitability, leverage, solvency, and activity sales to total assets. A study of 25 failed

firms predicted 24 a year ahead and only flagged 14 of 66 nonfailed firms as troubled. See Edward I. Altman, ''Financial Ratios, Discriminant Analysis, and the Prediction of Corporate Bankruptcy,'' *The Journal of Finance*, September 1968, pp. 589–609.

12. *Louis v. Pennsylvania Indus. Dev. Auth.*, 371 F. Supp. 877, 885 n. 14 (E.D. Pa 1974) cert. denied, 420 U.S. 993 (1974). Wanda A. Wallace, ''The Acceptability of Regression Analysis as Evidence in a Courtroom—Implications for the Auditor,'' *Auditing: A Journal of Practice & Theory* 2, no. 2 (Spring 1983), p. 81.

13. This is often referred to as the Hawthorne Effect, after the researcher whose experiment induced results for this very reason.

14. Quote by Sir Josiah Stamp, cited by George W. Downs and Patrick D. Larkey, *The Search for Government Efficiency: From Hubris to Helplessness* (Philadelphia: Temple University Press, 1986), p. 59.

15. Cited by George W. Downs and Patrick D. Larkey, *The Search for Government Efficiency: From Hubris to Helplessness* (Philadelphia: Temple University Press, 1986), p. 95.

16. Dewey was predicted to be the winner, but Truman prevailed.

17. Anthony G. Greenwald, ''Consequences of Prejudice Against the Null Hypothesis,'' *Psychological Bulletin*, January 1975, pp. 1–20.

18. Newton-Smith, as reported by Paul Danos, Doris L. Holt, and Andrew D. Bailey, Jr., ''The Interaction of Science and Attestation Standard Formation,'' *Auditing: A Journal of Practice & Theory*, Spring 1987, pp. 134–49.

19. Paul Danos, Doris L. Holt, and Andrew D. Bailey, Jr., ''The Interaction of Science and Attestation Standard Formation,'' *Auditing: A Journal of Practice & Theory*, Spring 1987, pp. 134–49.

20. M. Friedman, ''The Methodology of Positive Economics,'' in *Essays in Positive Economics* (Chicago: University of Chicago Press, 1953).

21. D. D. McClelland, ''Causal Explanation and Model Building in Economics,'' in *Causal Explanation and Model Building in History/Economics and the New Economic History* (Ithaca, N.Y.: Cornell University Press, 1975).

22. F. Andrews, L. Klem, T. Davidson, P. O'Malley, and W. L. Rodgers, *A Guide for Selecting Statistical Techniques for Analyzing Social Science Data*, 2nd ed. (Ann Arbor: University of Michigan, 1981).

23. Numerous examples are provided by F. Andrews, L. Klem, T. Davidson, P. O'Malley, and W. L. Rodgers, *A Guide for Selecting Statistical Techniques for Analyzing Social Science Data*, 2nd ed. (Ann Arbor: University of Michigan, 1981).

24. See, for example, Eric Noreen, ''An Empirical Comparison of Probit and OLS Regression Hypothesis Tests,'' *Journal of Accounting Research*, Spring 1988, pp. 119–33.

25. This is referred to as the Lauchenbruch or jackknife method if only one observation is omitted at a time.

26. Paul Danos, Doris L. Holt, and Andrew D. Bailey, Jr., "The Interaction of Science and Attestation Standard Formation," *Auditing: A Journal of Practice & Theory*, Spring 1987, pp. 134–49.

27. M. Friedman, "The Methodology of Positive Economics," in *Essays in Positive Economics* (Chicago: University of Chicago Press, 1953), p. 30.

28. James R. Boatsman, "Some Perspectives on Accounting Research," in *Perspectives on Research*, ed. R. Nair and T. Williams (Madison, Wisconsin: University of Wisconsin, 1980), pp. 1–12. Also, see Steven H. Cahn, *Saints and Scamps: Ethics in Academia* (Totowa, N.J.: Rowman & Littlefield, 1986), p. 39, for an account of Dr. Myron L. Fox and his address titled "Mathematical Game Theory as Applied to Physician Education." Not a single listener saw through the hoax despite the excessive use of double talk, non sequiturs, and contradictory statements!

29. Cited by George W. Downs and Patrick D. Larkey in *The Search for Government Efficiency: From Hubris to Helplessness* (Philadelphia: Temple University Press, 1986), p. 49.

30. William R. Kinney, Jr., "Commentary on 'The Relation of Accounting Research to Teaching and Practice: A 'Positive' View,' " *Accounting Horizons*, March 1989, p. 123.

31. For a review of such literature, see Tom Dyckman and Dale Morse, *Efficient Capital Markets & Accounting: A Critical Analysis* (Englewood Cliffs, N.J.: Prentice-Hall, 1986).

32. Richard F. Kochanek and Corine T. Norgaard, "Analyzing the Components of Operating Cash Flow: The Charter Company," *Accounting Horizons* 2, no. 1 (March 1988), pp. 58–66.

33. Amos Tversky and Daniel Kahneman, "Judgment Under Uncertainty: Heuristics and Biases," *Science* 185 (September 27, 1974), pp. 1124–31.

34. For further elaboration, see R. Libby, *Accounting and Human Information Processing: Theory and Applications* (Englewood Cliffs, N.J.: Prentice-Hall, 1981).

35. Amos Tversky and Daniel Kahneman, "The Framing of Decisions and the Psychology of Choice," *Science* 211 (January 30, 1981), pp. 453–58.

36. "Computers that Think Like People," *Fortune*, February 27, 1989, pp. 90–93.

37. S. F. Biggs and T. J. Mock, "Auditor Information Search Processes in the Evaluation of Internal Controls and Audit Scope Decisions," *Journal of Accounting Research*, Spring 1983, pp. 234–55.

38. Rick Antle and Joel S. Demski, "The Controllability Principle in Responsibility Accounting," *The Accounting Review* 63, no. 4 (October 1988), pp. 700–18.

39. William E. McCarthy, "Once Upon A Time at the Aglecap Store or Why Accountants of All Persuasions Need to Know About Economic Storytelling and Database Accounting," Michigan State University Working Paper, June 9, 1990, presented at the AAA Senior Faculty Consortium, Phoenix, Arizona, June 9, 1990.

40. William E. McCarthy, a professor at Michigan State University, offered this insight.

41. D. D. McClelland, "Causal Explanation and Model Building in Economics," in *Causal Explanation and Model Building in History/Economics and the New Economic History* (Ithaca, N.Y.: Cornell University Press, 1975).

42. "A Profile of a Researcher," *The Auditor's Report* 8, no. 1 (Fall 1984), pp. 1–3.

43. Cited by Arnold Wright, "Behavioral Research in Auditing: The State-of-the-Art," *The Auditor's Report* Vol. 11, no. 2 (Winter 1988), p. 3.

44. James Charlton, ed., *The Executive's Quotation Book: A Corporate Companion* (New York: St. Martin's Press, 1983).

45. David B. Montgomery and Donald G. Morrison, "A Note on Adjusting R^2," *The Journal of Finance* 28, no. 4 (September 1973), pp. 1009–13.

46. George A. Akerlof, "The Market for 'Lemons': Quality Uncertainty and the Market Mechanism," *Quarterly Journal of Economics* August 1970.

47. Wanda A. Wallace, *The Economic Role of the Audit in Free and Regulated Markets*, in *Auditing Monographs* (New York: Macmillan, 1984); also forthcoming from PWS-Kent (Boston, Mass.).

48. A discussion of means of avoiding Arrow's result can be found in James C. Gaa, *Methodological Foundations of Standard Setting for Corporate Financial Reporting*, Studies in Accounting Research, no. 28 (Sarasota, Fla.: American Accounting Association, 1988).

49. AICPA EDP Technology Research Subcommittee, "Expert Systems for Accountants: Has Their Time Come?" *Journal of Accountancy*, December 1987, pp. 117–25.

50. A. Tversky and D. Kahneman, "Judgment under Uncertainty: Heuristics and Biases," *Science* 185 (September 27, 1974), pp. 1124–31.

51. See James H. Lorie, Peter Dodd, and Mary Hamilton Kimpton, *The Stock Market: Theories and Evidence*, 2nd ed. (Homewood, Ill.: Richard D. Irwin, 1985), for further details.

52. See H. A. Simon, "A Behavioral Model of Rational Choice," *Quarterly Journal of Economics* 69 (February 1955), pp. 174–84 for a detailed discussion.

53. Described in Robert U. Ayres, *Technological Forecasting and Long-Range Planning* (New York: McGraw-Hill, 1969).

54. For elaboration, see Robert Libby, *Accounting and Human Information Processing: Theory and Applications* (Englewood Cliffs, N.J.: Prentice-Hall, 1981).

55. James C. Gaa, *Methodological Foundations of Standard Setting for Corporate Reporting*, Studies in Accounting Research, no. 28 (Sarasota, Fla.: American Accounting Association, 1988).

56. The implications of such a market for evaluation are explored by William H. Beaver in his book *Financial Reporting: An Accounting Revolution* (Englewood Cliffs, N.J.: Prentice-Hall, 1981).

57. R. Libby and R. K. Blashfield, "Performance of a Composite as a Function of the Number of Judges," *Organizational Behavior and Human Performance* 21 (April 1978), pp. 121–29.

58. A. H. Ashton and R. H. Ashton, "Sequential Belief Revision in Auditing," *The Accounting Review*, July 1988, pp. 623–41.

59. G. Shafer and R. Srivastava, "The Bayesian and Belief-Function Formalisms I: A General Perspective For Auditing," *Auditing: A Journal of Practice & Theory*, forthcoming.

60. Ron Copeland and Rob Ingram, *Municipal Financial Reporting and Disclosure Quality* (Reading, Mass.: Addison Wesley Publishing, 1983).

61. D. A. Leslie, A. Teitlebaum, and R. Anderson, *Dollar Unit Sampling* (Toronto: Copp Clark Pittman, 1979).

62. Keith C. Brown, "The Significance of Dummy Variables in Multiple Regressions Involving Financial and Economic Data," *The Journal of Finance* 23, no. 3 (June 1968), pp. 515–17; and Ronald F. Wippern, "Significance of Dummy Variables: Reply," *The Journal of Finance* 23, no. 3 (June 1968), pp. 518–19.

63. For an excellent discussion see Thomas R. Dyckman and Dale Morse, *Efficient Capital Markets and Accounting: A Critical Analysis*, 2nd ed. (Englewood Cliffs, N.J.: Prentice-Hall, 1986).

64. Michael T. Dugan and Keith A. Shriver, "The Importance of An Environmental Criterion in Applied Business Research," *Issues in Accounting Education*, Spring 1988, pp. 42–47.

65. David Burgstahler, "Inference from Empirical Research," *The Accounting Review*, January 1987, pp. 203–14; David Bakan, "The Test of Significance in Psychological Research," *Psychological Bulletin*, December 1966, pp. 423–37; and Anthony G. Greenwald, "Consequences of Prejudice Against the Null Hypothesis," *Psychological Bulletin*, January 1975, pp. 1–20.

66. Robert Schweitzer, "How Do Stock Returns React to Special Events?" *Business Review*, July–August 1989, pp. 17–27.

67. Hayes-Roth, "Knowledge-Based Expert Systems—The State of the Art in the U.S.," *Infotech*, Fall 1984, pp. 23–27.

68. See William H. Beaver, *Financial Reporting: An Accounting Revolution*, 2nd ed. (Englewood Cliffs, N.J.: Prentice-Hall, 1989), for further development of the effects of externalities.

69. Amos Tversky and Daniel Kahneman, "The Framing of Decisions and the Psychology of Choice," *Science* 211 (January 30, 1981), pp. 453–58.

70. L. Zadeh, *Information and Control*, June 1965, pp. 338–53 and "Fuzzy Sets as a Basis for a Theory of Possibility," *Fuzzy Sets and Systems*, 1 (1978), pp. 3–28.

71. Amos Tversky and Daniel Kahneman, "Belief in the Law of Small Numbers," *Psychological Bulletin*, 1971, pp. 105–10.

72. For an example in an auditing setting, see J. C. Fellingham and D. P. Newman, "Strategic Considerations in Auditing," *The Accounting Review*, October 1985, pp. 639–50.

73. N. Denzin, ed., *Sociological Methods: A Sourcebook* (New York: McGraw-Hill, 1978), cited by A. Rashad Abdel-Khalik and Bipin B. Ajinkya, *Empirical Research in Accounting: A Methodological Viewpoint* (Sarasota, Fla.: American Accounting Association, 1979), p. 17.

74. Robert H. Aston, Don N. Kleinmuntz, John B. Sullivan, and Lawrence A. Tomassini, "Audit Decision Making," in *Research Opportunities in Auditing: The Second Decade*, ed. A. Rashad Abdel-Khalik and Ira Solomon (Sarasota, Fla.: American Accounting Association, 1988).

75. Substantial development of this line of research is provided by John W. Buckley, Marlene H. Buckley, and Hung-Fu Chiang, *Research Methodology & Business Decisions* (New York: National Association of Accountants and the Society of Management Accountants of Canada, 1976).

76. For further details, see Baruch Lev, *Accounting & Information Theory*, Studies in Accounting Research, no. 2 (Sarasota, Fla.: American Accounting Association, 1969).

77. Joel S. Demski, *Information Analysis*, 2nd ed. (Reading, Mass.: Addison-Wesley, 1980); and A. Rashad Abdel-Khalik and Ira Solomon, eds., *Research Opportunities in Auditing: the Second Decade* (Sarasota, Fla.: American Accounting Association, 1988).

78. S. Siegel, *Nonparametric Statistics for Behavioral Sciences* (New York: McGraw-Hill, 1956), p. 239.

79. This definition was provided by Professor Gerald Salamon of Indiana University during a workshop at Texas A&M University.

80. L. Kohlberg, "Stages and Sequences: The Cognitive-Developmental Approach to Socialization," in *Handbook of Socialization Theory and Research*, ed. D. Goslin (Chicago: Rand McNally, 1969) pp. 347–480; and Levine Kohlberg and Hewer, "Moral Stages: A Current Formulation and a Response to Critics," in *Contributions to Human Development*, ed. E. Meachan, Vol. 10 (Basel, New York: Karger 1983).

81. S. Siegel, *Nonparametric Statistics for Behavioral Sciences* (New York: McGraw-Hill, 1956), p. 116.

82. Daniel Solow, *How to Read and Do Proofs: An Introduction to Mathematical Thought Process* (New York: John Wiley & Sons, 1982), p. 167.

83. See Kenneth J. Arrow and Hervé Raynaud, *Social Choice and Multicriterion Decision Making* (Cambridge: MIT Press, 1986), for a description of how to evaluate such problems.

84. See Richmond Campbell, "Background for the Uninitiated," in *Paradoxes of Rationality and Cooperation. Prisoner's Dilemma and Newcomb's Problem*, ed. Richmond Campbell and Lanning Sowden (Vancouver, B.C.: Iniversity of British Columbia Press, 1985), pp. 1–41.

85. Robert B. Thompson II, Chris Olsen, and J. Richard Dietrich, "The Influence of Estimation Period News Events on Standardized Market Model Prediction Errors," *The Accounting Review*, July, 1988 pp. 448–71.

86. S. Siegel, *Nonparametric Statistics for Behavioral Sciences* (New York: McGraw-Hill, 1956). A very useful reference in selecting the appropriate statistical technique for a given data set is F. M. Andrews, L. Klem, T. N. Davidson, P. M. O'Malley, and W. L. Rogers, *A Guide for Selecting Statistical Techniques* *for Analyzing Social Science Data*, 2nd ed. (Ann Arbor: University of Michigan, Institute for Social Science Research, 1981).

87. For elaboration on such matters, see Lauren Kelly-Newton, *Accounting Policy Formulation: The Role of Corporate Management (Reading, Massachusetts: Addison-Wesley Publishing, 1980).*

88. S. Siegel, *Nonparametric Statistics for the Behavioral Sciences* (New York: McGraw Hill, 1956).

89. See William H. Beaver, *Financial Reporting: An Accounting Revolution* (Engle-wood Cliffs, N.J.: Prentice-Hall, 1980) for an elaboration on the implications of such a concept.

90. Paul A. Griffin, *Research Report: Usefulness to Investors and Creditors of Information Provided by Financial Reporting*, 2nd Edition (Stamford, Conn.: Financial Accounting Standards Board, 1987).

91. For a description of various types of proofs, see Daniel Solow, *How to Read and Do Proofs: An Introduction to Mathematical Thought Process* (New York: John Wiley & Sons, 1982).

92. A. Tversky and D. Kahneman, "The Framing of Decisions and the Psychology of Choice," *Science* 211 (1981), pp. 453–58.

93. Amos Tversky and D. Kahneman, " The Framing of Decisions and the Psychology of Choice," *Science* 211 (January 30, 1981), pp. 453–58.

94. Numerous formal examples are provided by Donald T. Campbell and Julian C. Stanley, *Experimental and Quasi-Experimental Designs for Research* (Chicago: Rand McNally, 1963).

95. Amos Tversky and Daniel Kahneman, "Judgment Under Uncertainty: Heuristics and Biases," *Science* 185 (September 27, 1974), pp. 1124–31.

96. B. E. Cushing and J. K. Loebbecke, *Comparison of Audit Methodologies of Large Accounting Firms*, Studies in Accounting Research, no. 26 (Sarasota, Fla.: American Accounting Association, 1986).

97. Donald T. Campbell and Julian C. Stanley, *Experimental and Quasi-Experimental Designs for Research* (Chicago: Rand McNally, 1963).

98. Donald T. Campbell and Julian C. Stanley, *Experimental and Quasi-Experimental Designs for Research* (Chicago: Rand McNally, 1963).

99. Adapted from Daniel Solow, *How to Read and Do Proofs: An Introduction to Mathematical Thought Process* (New York: John Wiley & Sons, 1982).

100. Thomas R. Dyckman, "Commentary on Practice to Research—'What Have You Done for Me Lately?' " *Accounting Horizons*, March 1989, pp. 111–18.

101. Thomas R. Dyckman, "Commentary on Practice to Research—'What Have You Done for Me Lately?' " *Accounting Horizons*, March 1989, pp. 111–18.

102. See James C. Gaa, *Methodological Foundations of Standard Setting for Corporate Financial Reporting*, Studies in Accounting Research, no. 28 (Sarasota, Fla.: American Accounting Association, 1988).

103. William R. Kinney, Jr., "Empirical Accounting Research Design for Ph.D. Students," *The Accounting Review* 61, no. 2 (April 1986), pp. 338–50.

104. Amos Tversky and Daniel Kahneman, ''Belief in the Law of Small Numbers,'' *Psychological Bulletin*, 1971, pp. 105–10

105. Amos Tversky and Daniel Kahneman, '' The Framing of Decisions and the Psychology of Choice,'' *Science* 211 (January 30, 1981), pp. 453–58.

106. For related discussions, see Thomas R. Dyckman and Dale Morse, *Efficient Capital Markets and Accounting: A Critical Analysis*, 2nd ed. (Englewood Cliffs, N.J.: Prentice-Hall, 1986).

Key-Word Index

abnormal returns, 56
abstract, 48
accuracy, 36
Altman Z-score, 24
analytical research, 10
anchoring and adjustment, 59
appendices, 48
archival research, 10
asymmetrical information, 60
attribute sampling, 36
Bayesian decision theory, 59
between subjects, 16
case study, 10
Chi-square statistics, 41
compensatory models, 60
confidence level, 36
confirming evidence, 59
consensus, 60
control group, 18
controllability concept, 61
cost-benefit choice, 37
criteria for evaluation, 54
Delphi method, 10
derivative securities, 56
descriptive power, 43
directed sampling, 35
disconfirming evidence, 59
distribution, 41
Doctor Fox story, 45
double auction bidding, 62
earnings management, 57
efficient markets, 56
event, 56
expected error rate, 36
experimental markets, 62

experimental mortality, 18
external validity, 26
field study, 10, 61
footnotes, 48
full disclosure, 43
future research, 46
haphazard sampling, 35
history threats, 18
hold-out sample, 42
information content, 56
information transfer, 57
instrumentation, 15
interaction effect between selection criteria and
    maturation, 21
internal validity, 15
joint tests, 30
laboratory study, 10
Likert scale, 17
matched-sample approach, 22
maturation, 19
mean, 42
medians, 42
model-building process, 43
modeling techniques, 41
motivation of subjects, 31
multimethod approaches, 11
nominal data, 41
noncompensatory models, 60
nonparametric statistics, 42
nonrespondents, 41
normal distributions, 42
opinion research, 10
order effects, 19
ordinal, 7
parametric statistics, 42